. David   Frederic Remington   Goa
ssatt G. Courbet   H matisse   Eug
oussin J. F. Cropsey   Piet Mondriaan f
   J. Cole   J. Jor   Piero Paulo Rubens YVES
M Le Brun   P. Cezanne   Winslow Homer   f Bierstadt
   K   lr Jackson Pollock   W: van de velde
Joan Miró W: van de velde   Claude Monet
Poussin   H matisse   van Sargent
   modigliani   A. wey. th   Morgan
Picasso   Joshua Reynolds   YVES TANGUY.
ssatt P. Cezanne   Rembrandt Eug Delacroix
elacroix f Boucher   Frederic Remington Piero
odigliani J. F. Cropsey   M Le Brun J. Jor
A. wey. th   Vincent   A. VAN DYCK f Bie
   Boucher   Piero Paulo Rubens   mary Cassatt
Piet Mondriaan

ART · FARE

A Commemorative Celebration of Art & Food

Presented by The Toledo Museum of Art Aides

A R T · F A R E

A Commemorative Celebration of Art & Food

The cover:

STILL LIFE WITH PEAR

Blown glass objects, Flora Mace; stained alderwood bowl, Joey Kirkpatrick ©1994
Gift of Dale and Doug Anderson in honor of George and Dorothy Saxe
Handblown fruits—Bosc pear, Danish (acorn) squash, and eggplant—
rest on top of a hand-carved alderwood bowl
Photographer Tim Thayer

Published by the **Toledo Museum of Art Aides**
Copyright © 2000 by the **Toledo Museum of Art Aides**

Library of Congress Number: 00-131550
ISBN: 0-9678332-0-5

Designer: Dan Weeks, Weeks & Associates
Studio Photographer: Jim Rohman, Jim Rohman Photography
Food Stylist: Dianne S. Long, Long on Style
Archival Photographs: Toledo Museum of Art

Edited and Manufactured by Favorite Recipes® Press
an imprint of **FRP**™
P.O. Box 305142, Nashville, Tennessee 37230

Art Director: Steve Newman
Recipe Editor: Debbie Van Mol, RD
Project Coordinator: Tanis Westbrook
Managing Editor: Mary Cummings

Manufactured in the United States of America
First Printing: 2000   20,000 copies

For more information, or for additional copies of *Art Fare,* please contact:

TOLEDO MUSEUM OF ART AIDES

P. O. Box 1013
Toledo, Ohio 43697
419-255-8000 (7499)
800-644-6862 (7499)

CONTENTS

FOREWORD

The Toledo Museum of Art Aides need little introduction to those who will enjoy *ART FARE*. In fact, having known the Aides since their inception in 1957, I am aware that every task they undertake has been accomplished with loving care, understanding, skill, thoughtfulness, and good common sense. I am confident the recipes in this beautiful cookbook will be well worth presentation to your family and friends.

Now, as the Toledo Museum of Art reaches its centennial year in 2001 (The Metropolitan Museum of Art in New York and The Museum of Fine Arts, Boston, are only 25 years older), it is wise to mention that our museum has always been known for its pioneering educational programs.

Much of this reputation is based on the declaration in 1901 by the Museum's founder, Edward Drummond Libbey, and his wife, Florence Scott Libbey, that the Museum must belong to ALL in the community and that free education in art and music should be offered to our children by the Museum. This far-sighted innovative concept has resulted in the astonishing growth in membership and in many other Museum programs that were carried out on a completely volunteer basis by intensely loyal groups, the Museum Docents, and, later, the Art Museum Aides.

I don't think any of us in 1957 possessed the vision that the Art Museum Aides program would grow and develop as it has, nor that the range of original activities would have been so varied and effectively implemented by the aides for the ongoing development of the Museum.

Now, as the Toledo Museum of Art enters its second century, we hope that all will enjoy, learn from, and benefit from our beloved Museum and that this splendid cookbook will give you comfort and joy.

Otto Wittmann

Otto Wittmann
Director Emeritus

AN APPRECIATION

The Art Museum Aides' choice of a cookbook to salute the Museum's Centennial is a perfect one. While this cookbook reflects this volunteer group's sense of community, it also reminds us that in its highest expression, the art of the table appeals to the eye, as well as to the senses of taste and smell.

Complementing the recipes are images from the Museum's splendid collection, including a seventeenth-century Dutch still life painting, cut-glass Libbey punch bowl, a silver tureen, and a gilded bronze centerpiece. The recipes, and indeed this entire cookbook project, have been held to similar standards of creativity and craftsmanship.

We thank the Aides for their more than forty years of exceptional devotion to the Museum and extend enthusiastic congratulations and gratitude for this most-recent expression of their commitment.

Roger M. Berkowitz

Director

The Toledo Museum of Art

Table centerpieces or "surtouts de table" were an innovation introduced at Versailles in the 1690s and quickly adopted at other European courts. Designed as platforms on which containers for condiments, spices, or fruit were conveniently arranged, these centerpieces remained standard items on grand dining tables well into the nineteenth century.

TABLE CENTERPIECE
Gilded bronze and marble veneer about 1710

Gift of Mr. and Mrs. Edward H. Alexander

THE LIBBEY LEGACY

Edward Drummond Libbey arrived in Toledo from New England in 1888 with a strong and loyal band of 250 glass workers and their families. They were met by Mayor James K. Hamilton and paraded to the new factory site. Libbey's decision to establish his glass factory in Toledo was based on the enormous deposits of sand with a high silica content and the opening of the midwest gas fields that would supply the fuel for the glass furnaces. It proved to be a wise and providential decision for the factory location.

By 1901, Edward Drummond Libbey had become a successful entrepreneur in the glass industry. This man of intellectual curiosity and a passion for the arts realized that something was missing in his OWN life and in that of industrial Toledo. Believing profoundly in education and concerned about how the aesthetic needs of the community could be met, he conceived the idea of bringing art and beauty to the city of Toledo.

Mr. Libbey convened a group of business leaders and artists in 1901, and the Toledo Museum of Art was born. It opened to the public using a few rented rooms in downtown Toledo, where visitors could view a mummified Egyptian cat and a painting of sheep crossing a meadow. By 1908, the Museum outgrew its original space.

Mr. Libbey then envisioned the philanthropic idea of a matching funds program for erecting a new Museum building by donating $50,000 in cash if the community would raise the other $50,000. The campaign achieved its goal in less than a month. Even the schoolchildren of the city donated their pennies, nickels, and dimes.

Mr. Libbey's wife, Florence Scott Libbey, provided the land for this new building, and, in 1912, our Museum opened its doors.

Mr. Libbey once said: "The only enjoyment and pleasure in life is in the service of giving ... whatever I have done is because of that." With this inspired vision and generous endowments provided by the Libbeys, the Toledo Museum of Art and its distinguished collection have become highly respected and world renowned.

Above: Edward Drummond Libbey and Florence Scott Libbey

At right (clockwise), selections of Toledo Treasures purchased with funds from the Libbey Endowment:

Exekias, *Amphora and Lid,* 550–530 B.C.
Portrait Bust of the Emperor Domitian,
    about 90
Henri Matisse, *Apollo,* 1953 (Detail)
Piero di Cosimo, *Adoration of the Child,*
    about 1495–1500
Peter Paul Rubens, *The Crowning of St.*
    Catherine, 1631
Joan Miro, *Woman Haunted by the Passage*
    of the Bird-Dragonfly Omen of Bad News,
    1938 (Detail)
Pablo Picasso, *Woman with a Crow,* 1904
James Tissot, *London Visitors,* 1874 (Detail)

he Monroe Street facade of the Toledo
Museum of Art—This view focuses on the main
entrance to the original core of the building,
designed in the Neoclassical style by Edward B.
Green of the firm Green & Wicks. Inaugurated
in 1912, and expanded in 1926 and 1933,

The Center for the Visual Arts of
The University of Toledo—Seen here from
the intersection of Monroe Street and
Collingwood Boulevard, the building was
designed by Frank O. Gehry and Associates,
Inc., and completed in 1992. The metal and
glass surfaces contrast with and complement
the Museum's marble facade.

*The recipes featured here
are Crab Cakes with Red
Pepper Aïoli, Tortilla Spirals,
and Mussels on the Half
Shell with Pesto.*

Summer Mint Delight

SERVES 36

3 cups sugar
3 cups water
1 (6-ounce) can frozen orange juice concentrate
1 (6-ounce) can frozen lemonade concentrate
2 cups whole fresh mint leaves
Ginger ale, chilled

Bring the sugar and water to a boil in a saucepan. Stir in the orange juice concentrate, lemonade concentrate and snipped mint. Remove from heat. Let stand for 1 hour; strain. Pour into an airtight container. Store in the refrigerator for up to 2 months.

For each serving, combine 2 tablespoons of the syrup with 1 cup ginger ale. Pour over crushed ice in a glass. Garnish with mint leaves.

Blue Ridge Tea

SERVES 16

6 tea bags
1 quart boiling water
1 (6-ounce) can frozen lemonade concentrate
1 (6-ounce) can frozen limeade concentrate
$1/2$ to $3/4$ cup sugar

Steep the tea bags in the boiling water in a heatproof bowl for 5 minutes; discard the tea bags. Add the lemonade concentrate, limeade concentrate and sugar, stirring until the sugar dissolves. Pour into a 1-gallon container. Add enough cold water to fill the container and mix well. Pour over ice in glasses. Garnish with lemon or lime slices.

Pears with Parmesan Cream

SERVES 6

1 loaf Italian bread
$3^{1}/2$ cups freshly grated Parmigiano-Reggiano cheese
2 cups plus 2 tablespoons heavy cream
$1/8$ teaspoon freshly ground white pepper
3 firm Bosc or Anjou pears, peeled
6 small bunches grapes
1 tablespoon balsamic vinegar, or to taste

Preheat the oven to 300 degrees. Cut the bread diagonally into 18 slices approximately 2 inches in diameter and $1/4$ inch thick. Arrange the slices in a single layer on a baking sheet. Place the baking sheet on the bottom oven rack. Bake for 25 to 35 minutes or until golden brown. Let stand at room temperature for 24 hours.

Combine the cheese, heavy cream and white pepper in a double boiler over boiling water. Cook for 5 minutes or until smooth, stirring constantly. Remove from heat. Pour into a shallow ovenproof glass dish. Cool slightly. Chill, covered, for 12 hours.

Cut the pears lengthwise into halves. Cut 1 pear half into thin slices. Fan on a chilled plate. Repeat the process with the remaining pear halves. Spoon a heaping spoonful of the Parmesan cream at the base of each fan. Arrange some of the grapes and 3 slices of the bread in a decorative pattern on the plate. Drizzle the balsamic vinegar over the Parmesan cream. Serve immediately.

Brie Baked en Croûte with Tomato Chutney

SERVES 15 TO 20

Tomato Chutney
1 (28-ounce) can chopped tomatoes
1 large onion, chopped
1/2 cup sugar
1/2 cup cider vinegar
1/3 cup currants
Grated zest of 1 lemon
1 1/2 teaspoons mustard seeds
1/2 teaspoon salt
1/4 teaspoon cayenne pepper
1/4 teaspoon allspice
1/4 teaspoon cinnamon
Brie
1 (17-ounce) package frozen puff pastry, thawed
1 (8-ounce) round Brie cheese, cut horizontally into halves
1 egg, beaten

For the chutney, combine the undrained tomatoes, onion, sugar, vinegar, currants, lemon zest, mustard seeds, salt, cayenne pepper, allspice and cinnamon in a saucepan and mix well. Cook over medium heat for 30 minutes, stirring occasionally; reduce heat. Simmer until thickened, stirring occasionally. Remove from heat. Store leftovers, covered, in the refrigerator for up to 3 months.

For the Brie, roll 1 sheet of the pastry into a 1/8-inch-thick 15-inch round on a lightly floured surface. Using the Brie as a guide, cut a round the size of the cheese out of the remaining pastry sheet. Cut 5 stars from the pastry trimmings using a 2 3/4-inch star cutter.

Arrange the larger of the pastry rounds in a shallow baking pan. Place the bottom half of the Brie cut side up in the center of the pastry. Spread 1/2 cup of the chutney to within 1/2 inch of the edge of the cheese. Top with the remaining Brie half cut side down. Bring the pastry up to enclose the Brie, leaving a 1-inch border; do not stretch the pastry. Brush the border with some of the egg. Top with the remaining pastry, pressing the edge gently to seal. Brush with the remaining egg.

Arrange the pastry stars in a decorative pattern over the top. Chill for 30 minutes. Preheat the oven to 425 degrees. Bake on the middle oven rack for 20 to 40 minutes or until puffed and golden brown. Serve with the remaining Tomato Chutney and assorted party crackers and/or sliced French bread.

Holiday Brie

SERVES 6 TO 8

Cranberry Relish
1/2 unpeeled orange
1 cup (heaping) cranberries
6 tablespoons packed brown sugar
3 tablespoons sliced almonds
1 teaspoon Grand Marnier
1/8 teaspoon nutmeg
Brie
1 small round Brie cheese, about 34 ounces

For the relish, remove the seeds and membranes from the orange. Process the orange in a food processor until finely chopped. Process the cranberries in a food processor until of relish consistency. Add the orange, brown sugar, almonds, Grand Marnier and nutmeg. Pulse 3 or 4 times or until of the desired consistency. May prepare in advance and store, covered, in the refrigerator.

For the Brie, preheat the oven to 500 degrees. Arrange the Brie in a baking dish. Spread the top of the Brie with the relish. Bake for 4 to 5 minutes. Garnish with grapes and/or fresh fruit. Serve with wafers.

Brie and Wild Mushroom Fondue

SERVES 4 TO 6

1 ounce dried porcini mushrooms
1 cup boiling water
8 ounces fresh shiitake mushrooms, finely chopped
2 tablespoons butter
2 tablespoons chopped shallots
1 cup dry white wine
1 (16-ounce) Brie cheese round, rind removed, chopped
2 tablespoons cornstarch
Salt and pepper to taste

Combine the porcini mushrooms and boiling water in a heatproof bowl. Let stand for 20 minutes. Drain, reserving the liquid. Strain the liquid, discarding the solids. Chop the mushrooms. Sauté the shiitake mushrooms in the butter in a skillet over medium heat for 3 minutes or until tender. Stir in the shallots. Sauté for 1 minute.

Stir in the porcini mushrooms and reserved liquid; increase heat to high. Simmer for 3 minutes or until the liquid is absorbed, stirring frequently. Stir in the wine. Simmer over medium heat, stirring occasionally.

Toss the cheese and cornstarch in a bowl until the cheese is coated. Add the cheese mixture to the mushroom mixture in 3 batches, mixing well after each addition. Simmer until the cheese melts and the mixture just begins to simmer, stirring frequently; do not boil. Season with salt and pepper. Serve with French bread cubes, steamed asparagus spears, steamed green beans, steamed quartered new red potatoes and/or cooked cubed chicken.

Feta with Pepper Honey

SERVES 16

2^1/$_2$ teaspoons black peppercorns
1 pound feta cheese
Red leaf lettuce
^{1}/$_3$ cup honey

Crack the peppercorns using a mortar and pestle or the bottom of a heavy skillet. Rinse the feta cheese and drain. Pat dry with paper towels. Cut the feta cheese thinly into single serving portions. Arrange in a decorative pattern on a serving platter lined with red leaf lettuce.

Combine the cracked peppercorns and honey in a measuring cup and mix well. Drizzle over the feta cheese. Serve with assorted party crackers and/or toasted baguette slices.

Feta Fetish

SERVES 25

8 ounces cream cheese, chopped, softened
^{3}/$_4$ cup (1^1/$_2$ sticks) butter, chopped, softened
6 ounces feta cheese, crumbled
1 garlic clove, finely chopped
^{1}/$_4$ teaspoon oregano
1 bunch green onions, sliced, chopped
1 (4-ounce) can chopped black olives, drained
1 or 2 tomatoes, chopped

Process the cream cheese, butter and feta cheese in a food processor until smooth. Add the garlic and oregano. Process until blended. Mound on a serving platter. Sprinkle with the green onions. Arrange the olives and tomatoes around the outer edge of the cheese. Serve with assorted party crackers and/or toasted pita wedges.

Bacon Cheese Crisps

MAKES 3 DOZEN CRISPS

2 cups shredded Cheddar cheese
1/2 cup (1 stick) butter, softened
1 teaspoon Worcestershire sauce
1/4 teaspoon salt
1/4 teaspoon dry mustard
3 drops of Tabasco sauce
1 1/4 cups flour
10 slices crisp-cooked bacon, crumbled

Beat the cheese and butter in a mixing bowl until blended. Add the Worcestershire sauce, salt, dry mustard and Tabasco sauce and mix well. Stir in the flour and bacon. Shape the dough into 2 logs 1 1/2 inches in diameter. Chill, covered, in the refrigerator.

Preheat the oven to 375 degrees. Cut the logs into 1/8- to 1/4-inch slices. Arrange the slices on a baking sheet. Bake for 8 to 10 minutes or until light brown. Remove to a wire rack to cool.

Variation: May substitute 1 cup crisp rice cereal for the crumbled bacon.

Basil Chèvre Spread

MAKES 1 CUP

8 ounces goat cheese or herb goat cheese
1/2 to 3/4 cup chopped fresh basil leaves
2 teaspoons basil-infused olive oil
1 large garlic clove, minced

Process the goat cheese, basil, olive oil and garlic in a food processor until smooth. Serve with breadsticks and/or toasted Italian bread.

Note: May prepare up to 3 days in advance and store, covered, in the refrigerator.

Chèvre-Stuffed Mushrooms

SERVES 10

24 large mushrooms
2 tablespoons chopped onion
1/3 cup butter
3/4 cup bread crumbs
2 tablespoons chopped fresh parsley
2 tablespoons lemon juice
1 teaspoon salt
3 ounces chèvre, crumbled
2 ounces bleu cheese, crumbled

Remove the stems from the mushrooms. Chop the stems. Arrange the mushrooms cap side down in a greased 9×13-inch baking dish. Sauté the mushroom stems and onion in the butter in a skillet until tender. Stir in the bread crumbs, parsley, lemon juice and salt. Cool to room temperature.

Preheat the oven to 450 degrees. Add the chèvre and bleu cheese to the bread crumb mixture and mix well. Spoon the bread crumb mixture into the mushroom caps. Bake for 7 to 10 minutes or until light brown.

Note: May prepare the bread crumb mixture 1 day in advance and store, covered, in the refrigerator.

*T*he ancient Greeks never drank undiluted wine, but rather, mixed it with water in large vessels called kraters. This example is notable for its sheer size and finely painted figural scenes.

The Creusa Painter
Greek, South Italian, Lucanian

VOLUTE KRATER
Earthenware, 400–380 B.C.

Purchased with funds from the Libbey Endowment, Gift of Edward Drummond Libbey

Crab and Shrimp Crostini

MAKES 40 CROSTINI

1/2 cup bottled clam juice
10 ounces medium shrimp, peeled, deveined
1 cup thinly sliced green onions
2/3 cup mayonnaise
4 teaspoons fresh lemon juice
2 garlic cloves, finely chopped
1 teaspoon Hungarian paprika
1/2 teaspoon cayenne pepper
8 ounces crab meat, flaked
Salt and pepper to taste
40 (1/4-inch) slices French bread or sourdough baguette
1/3 cup olive oil

Bring the clam juice to a simmer in a large skillet over medium heat. Add the shrimp. Simmer, covered, until the shrimp turn pink, turning once. Remove the shrimp with a slotted spoon to a cutting board and coarsely chop, reserving the liquid.

Bring the reserved liquid to a boil. Boil for 2 minutes or until reduced to 2 tablespoons. Let stand until cool. Combine the green onions, mayonnaise, lemon juice, garlic, paprika and cayenne pepper in a bowl and mix well. Stir in the shrimp, reserved cooking liquid and crab meat. Season with salt and pepper.

Preheat the oven to 375 degrees. Brush both sides of the bread with the olive oil. Arrange the slices in a single layer on a baking sheet. Bake for 4 minutes or until crisp and golden brown on both sides. Let stand until cool.

Spread each slice with some of the shrimp mixture. Arrange the crostini on a serving platter. Garnish with lemon wedges and additional thinly sliced green onions. Serve immediately.

Hot Ryes

MAKES 3 DOZEN

1 cup finely shredded Swiss cheese
1 (4-ounce) can chopped black olives, drained
1/4 cup crumbled crisp-cooked bacon
1/4 cup minced green onions or chives
1/4 cup mayonnaise
1 teaspoon Worcestershire sauce
36 slices party rye bread

Preheat the oven to 375 degrees. Combine the cheese, olives, bacon and green onions in a bowl and mix well. Stir in the mayonnaise and Worcestershire sauce.

Arrange the bread slices in a single layer on a baking sheet. Spread the cheese mixture over the slices. Bake for 10 to 15 minutes or until brown and bubbly. Serve immediately.

Swiss Artichoke Puffs

MAKES 30 PUFFS

3/4 cup mayonnaise
1 cup freshly grated Parmesan cheese
1 tablespoon chopped fresh parsley
1/4 teaspoon onion powder
1/4 teaspoon Worcestershire sauce
1 loaf party rye, toasted
1 (14-ounce) can artichoke hearts, drained, cut into quarters
Swiss cheese, thinly sliced, cut into quarters

Combine the mayonnaise, cheese, parsley, onion powder and Worcestershire sauce in a bowl and mix well. Spread the mayonnaise mixture over 1 side of each bread slice. Arrange on a baking sheet. Top each slice with an artichoke quarter and cheese quarter. Broil until the cheese melts. Serve immediately

Warm Spinach and Parmesan Spread

MAKES 3 CUPS

2 tablespoons butter
2 tablespoons olive oil
1 3/4 cups chopped onions
6 large garlic cloves, minced
2 tablespoons flour
1/2 cup chicken broth
1/2 cup heavy cream
10 ounces baby spinach, stems removed
1 cup (heaping) grated Parmesan cheese
1/4 cup sour cream
1/2 teaspoon cayenne pepper
Salt and black pepper to taste
Baguette slices, toasted or untoasted

Heat the butter and olive oil in a heavy saucepan over medium heat until the butter melts. Add the onions and garlic. Sauté for 10 minutes or until the onions are tender. Stir in the flour. Cook for 3 minutes, stirring constantly. Whisk in the broth and heavy cream gradually. Bring to a boil, stirring constantly. Cook for 4 minutes or until thickened, stirring frequently. Remove from heat. Stir in the spinach, cheese, sour cream and cayenne pepper. Season with salt and black pepper. Spoon into a serving bowl. Garnish with fresh parsley. Serve warm with baguette slices.

Sicilian Salsa

SERVES 8 TO 10

12 ounces California black olives, chopped
2 ounces green olives, chopped
2 ounces kalamata olives, chopped
1 ounce fresh basil leaves, minced
6 to 10 garlic cloves, minced
$1/2$ to $3/4$ cup olive oil
Pepper to taste

Combine the olives, basil, garlic, olive oil and pepper in a bowl and mix gently. Serve in a crock surrounded with toasted baguette slices. Garnish with slivers of roasted red pepper and fresh basil.

Bistro Roasted Garlic

SERVES 10 TO 12

4 medium garlic heads
$1/4$ cup olive oil

Preheat the oven to 350 degrees. Remove the top of each garlic head with a sharp knife, exposing the cloves. Arrange the heads cut side up in a shallow baking dish. Brush with the olive oil. Add enough water to the baking dish to measure 1 inch. Bake, covered, for 45 to 60 minutes or until the garlic is soft enough to spread and light brown. Serve with baguette slices.

Gauguin's Coconut Chicken

SERVES 8

Plum Sauce
1 jar plum jelly
$1/4$ cup fresh orange juice
1 tablespoon sherry
Chicken
$1/2$ cup milk
1 egg, beaten
$1/2$ cup plus 2 tablespoons flour
$1^1/2$ teaspoons seasoned salt
$1/2$ teaspoon white pepper
2 boneless skinless chicken breasts, cut into bite-size pieces
1 (7-ounce) package shredded coconut
Peanut oil for deep-frying

For the sauce, whisk the jelly in a bowl until frothy. Add the orange juice and wine gradually, whisking constantly until blended.

For the chicken, whisk the milk and egg in a bowl until blended. Stir in the flour, seasoned salt and white pepper. Dip the chicken in the egg mixture. Coat with the coconut.

Deep-fry the chicken in the peanut oil in a skillet until golden brown; drain. Serve from a heated tray or chafing dish with the Plum Sauce.

Note: May prepare the chicken in advance and store, covered, in the refrigerator. Reheat in a 400-degree oven for 5 minutes.

Pine Nut Dolmades with Yogurt Feta Dip

SERVES 40

Dolmades

1 (14-ounce) can diced tomatoes
1 cup long grain rice
1 cup sliced green onions
1/2 cup packed finely chopped fresh mint
1/2 cup pine nuts, toasted
1/2 cup extra-virgin olive oil
2 large garlic cloves, minced
Salt and pepper to taste
52 grape leaves (one 2-pound jar)
1/4 cup fresh lemon juice

Yogurt Feta Dip

1 cup plain yogurt
4 ounces feta cheese, crumbled
1 large green onion, cut into 1-inch pieces
1/4 teaspoon grated lemon zest

For the dolmades, combine the undrained tomatoes, rice, green onions, mint, pine nuts, olive oil and garlic in a bowl and mix well. Season with salt and pepper.

Rinse the grape leaves with cold water; drain. Line the bottom of a large Dutch oven with 6 of the grape leaves. Place 1 grape leaf vein side up on a work surface. Cut off the stem. Place 1 tablespoon of the rice mixture in the center of the leaf. Fold the sides over the filling. Roll tightly starting at the stem end to enclose the filling. Arrange seam side down in the prepared Dutch oven. Repeat the process with 39 of the remaining grape leaves, layering the dolmades as soon as the bottom of the Dutch oven is covered. Drizzle with the lemon juice. Cover with the remaining 6 grape leaves. Add just enough water to the Dutch oven to almost cover the dolmades. Place a heatproof plate over the top to weigh down the dolmades; cover.

Bring to a boil; reduce heat to low. Simmer for 35 minutes or until the rice is tender and most of the liquid is absorbed. Remove from heat; drain. Chill, covered, in the refrigerator. May prepare up to 2 days in advance and store, covered, in the refrigerator.

For the dip, combine the yogurt, cheese, green onion and lemon zest in a food processor container. Process until almost smooth. Chill, covered, in the refrigerator. Serve with the dolmades.

Mushrooms in Phyllo

MAKES 30

1/4 cup sherry
2 tablespoons olive oil
1 tablespoon balsamic vinegar
1 shallot, finely chopped
1/4 teaspoon salt
12 to 16 ounces mushrooms, coarsely chopped
30 frozen phyllo tart shells, thawed
6 ounces Brie cheese, rind removed, thinly sliced

Preheat the oven to 350 degrees. Combine the sherry, olive oil, balsamic vinegar, shallot and salt in a small skillet. Sauté for 5 minutes or until the liquid is absorbed and the shallot is tender. Stir in the mushrooms.

Arrange the tart shells on a baking sheet. Place some of the Brie cheese in each shell. Spoon the mushroom mixture into the prepared shells. Bake for 8 minutes. Serve immediately.

Note: May prepare the mushroom mixture in advance and store, covered, in the refrigerator.

Tortilla Spirals

SERVES 20

2 cups boursin cheese, softened
1/4 cup mayonnaise
8 (10-inch) sun-dried tomato tortillas or flour tortillas
2 cups grated carrots
1 cup watercress leaves
1 cup finely chopped yellow bell pepper
1/2 cup grated red onion
2 tablespoons finely chopped fresh parsley
1/4 teaspoon ground pepper

Combine the boursin and mayonnaise in a bowl and mix until blended. Spread 1 side of each tortilla with some of the cheese mixture. Toss the carrots, watercress, bell pepper, onion, parsley and pepper in a bowl. Sprinkle evenly over the cheese mixture. Roll tightly to enclose the filling.

Cut the tortilla rolls into slices using this decorative presentation. Make the first cut a straight cut, the second cut at a slight angle, the third cut straight, the fourth cut at a slight angle. Repeat the process until all the tortilla rolls are sliced. This gives each slice a flat bottom and an angled top cut.

Bacon-Wrapped Shrimp

MAKES 2 DOZEN

Creamy Horseradish Sauce
8 ounces cream cheese, softened
1/2 cup mayonnaise
1/2 cup sour cream
3 tablespoons prepared horseradish
1 tablespoon fresh lemon juice
Tabasco sauce to taste
Salt and freshly ground white pepper to taste
Shrimp
24 large shrimp, peeled, deveined
24 whole water chestnuts, drained
12 thin slices bacon, cut vertically into halves
6 tablespoons unsalted butter

For the sauce, beat the cream cheese in a mixing bowl until smooth. Add the mayonnaise, sour cream, horseradish, lemon juice, Tabasco sauce, salt and white pepper. Beat until blended.

For the shrimp, wrap each shrimp around 1 water chestnut. Wrap each with a bacon half and secure with a wooden pick. Heat 3 tablespoons of the butter in a large heavy skillet over high heat. Add half the shrimp. Cook for 2 1/2 minutes per side or until the bacon browns. Transfer the shrimp to a gratin dish. Repeat the process with the remaining butter and remaining shrimp. May be prepared in advance to this point and stored, covered, in the refrigerator.

Preheat the broiler. Spoon the sauce into a pastry tube. Pipe in a decorative pattern over the shrimp or spoon the sauce over the shrimp. Broil until golden brown. Serve immediately.

Note: Preheat heavy skillet before adding butter to prevent burning.

olors of Italy—
A tri-color triumph

Simply Shrimp

SERVES 10

1 medium onion
4 cups mayonnaise
Juice of 1 lemon
Salt and pepper to taste
Dillweed to taste
2 to 3 pounds large shrimp, cooked, peeled, deveined

Grate the onion into a bowl. Add the mayonnaise, lemon juice, salt, pepper and dillweed and mix well. Stir in the shrimp. Marinate, covered, in the refrigerator for 24 hours, stirring occasionally. Spoon into a glass serving bowl. Garnish with sprigs of fresh parsley. Serve with wooden picks.

Savory Palmiers

MAKES 2 DOZEN

1 (17-ounce) package frozen puff pastry, thawed
$1/2$ cup honey mustard
1 pound thinly sliced ham
$1/2$ cup grated Parmesan cheese
1 egg
1 tablespoon water

Preheat the oven to 400 degrees. Roll 1 sheet of the puff pastry on a lightly floured surface. Spread with half the honey mustard. Top with half the ham. Sprinkle with half the Parmesan cheese. Roll up the 2 short sides to meet in the center. Turn over and cut into $1/2$-inch slices. Repeat the process with the remaining pastry, honey mustard, ham and cheese. Arrange the slices cut side down 2 inches apart on a baking sheet lined with parchment paper. Brush with a mixture of the egg and water. Bake for 10 to 12 minutes or until light brown.

Cheddar Cloud

SERVES 20 TO 30

2 cups ricotta cheese
2 cups shredded Cheddar cheese
1 medium onion, finely chopped
2 eggs, lightly beaten
$1/2$ teaspoon salt
$1/4$ teaspoon cayenne pepper
1 (17-ounce) package frozen puff pastry, thawed

Preheat the oven to 375 degrees. Combine the ricotta cheese, Cheddar cheese, onion, eggs, salt and cayenne pepper in a bowl and mix well. Place 1 sheet of the puff pastry on a 10×15-inch baking sheet. Spread with the cheese mixture. Top with the remaining pastry sheet. Bake for 40 to 50 minutes or until golden brown. Let cool slightly. Cut into squares. Serve immediately.

Spicy Glazed Pecans

SERVES 10 TO 12

$1/2$ cup sugar
3 tablespoons water
1 teaspoon (scant) salt
$1/4$ to $1/2$ teaspoon cayenne pepper
3 cups pecan halves

Preheat the oven to 350 degrees. Combine the sugar, water, salt and cayenne pepper in a saucepan and mix well. Bring to a boil over medium heat, stirring frequently. Boil for 2 minutes. Add the pecans, stirring until coated. Spread the pecans evenly on a buttered baking sheet. Bake for 10 to 15 minutes or just until the pecans begin to brown. Transfer the pecans to a baking sheet lined with parchment paper and separate with a fork. Let stand until cool. Store in an airtight container for up to 1 week.

Crab Cakes with Red Pepper Aïoli

MAKES 35 SERVINGS

Red Pepper Aïoli
1 cup mayonnaise
6 roasted red bell pepper strips
2 garlic cloves, crushed
Tabasco sauce and lemon juice to taste
Salt and pepper to taste
Crab Cakes
3 cans lump crab meat, drained, flaked
1/2 cup seafood-seasoned bread crumbs
1/2 cup minced fresh cilantro
1/2 each red and yellow bell pepper, chopped
4 scallions, minced
1 egg, beaten
1 garlic clove, minced
1 jalapeño chile, minced
1/4 to 1/2 cup mayonnaise
Tabasco sauce to taste
Salt and pepper to taste
1/4 cup seafood-seasoned bread crumbs
Butter

For the sauce, combine the mayonnaise, roasted bell pepper, garlic, Tabasco sauce, lemon juice, salt and pepper in a food processor container. Pulse until blended and of the desired consistency. Chill, covered, in the refrigerator.

For the crab cakes, combine the crab meat, 1/2 cup bread crumbs, cilantro, bell peppers, scallions, egg, garlic and chile in a bowl and mix well. Stir in mayonnaise just until the mixture adheres. Season with Tabasco sauce, salt and pepper. Chill, covered, in the refrigerator.

Shape the crab meat mixture into 35 silver-dollar size cakes. Coat with 1/4 cup bread crumbs. Panfry the cakes in butter in a skillet until brown on both sides; drain. Arrange the crab cakes on a baking sheet. Chill, covered, until just before serving. Reheat at 400 degrees for 10 minutes. Serve with the sauce.

Mussels on the Half Shell with Pesto

SERVES 20

Mussels
40 mussels
1 cup dry white wine
1 cup water
1/4 cup chopped shallots
2 tablespoons white wine vinegar
4 garlic cloves, crushed
Pesto
4 cups fresh basil leaves
4 garlic cloves
3 tablespoons olive oil
6 tablespoons freshly grated Parmesan cheese
2 tablespoons mayonnaise
Salt and pepper to taste

For the mussels, scrub, soak and debeard the mussels; drain. Bring the wine, water, shallots, wine vinegar and 4 crushed garlic cloves to a boil in a stockpot. Add the mussels in batches to the stockpot. Cook, covered, for 4 minutes or until the mussels open. Transfer the mussels with a slotted spoon to a large bowl. Let stand until cool. Strain the cooking liquid, reserving 1 cup.

Remove the mussels from the shells, reserving half of each shell. Transfer the mussels to a bowl. Chill the mussels and reserved shells, covered, in the refrigerator.

For the pesto, combine the basil and 4 garlic cloves in a food processor container. Process until finely chopped. Add 3/4 cup of the reserved cooking liquid and olive oil. Process until blended. Add the cheese and mayonnaise and process, adding the remaining 1/4 cup reserved cooking liquid if needed for a pesto consistency. Transfer the pesto to a bowl. Season with salt and pepper. Add the mussels and toss to coat.

Chill, covered, for 1 hour or for up to 1 day. Spoon the mussel mixture into the reserved shells. Arrange on a serving platter. Garnish with sprigs of fresh basil.

Caponata

SERVES 8 TO 12

Sprigs of fresh parsley and thyme
Celery leaves
2 medium onions, thinly sliced
1/4 cup olive oil
Salt to taste
2 red bell peppers, thinly sliced
2 cups chopped fresh tomatoes
4 medium garlic cloves, thinly sliced
1/4 cup olive oil
8 ribs celery with leaves, chopped
2 teaspoons fresh thyme leaves
1/2 cup olive oil
1 medium unpeeled eggplant, chopped
1/2 cup red wine vinegar
2 tablespoons sugar
1 cup drained pitted green olives
1/4 cup rinsed drained capers

Tie the parsley, thyme and celery leaves with kitchen twine to form a bundle. Combine the onions, 1/4 cup olive oil and salt in a skillet. Cook over low heat for 5 minutes, stirring frequently. Stir in the bell peppers. Cook for 5 minutes, stirring frequently. Add the tomatoes and mix well. Cook for 5 minutes, stirring occasionally. Add the herb bundle and garlic and mix well. Cook, covered, over low heat for 20 minutes or until the vegetables are tender but firm, stirring occasionally. Remove from heat and discard the herb bundle.

Heat 1/4 cup olive oil in a skillet until hot. Add the celery. Cook over medium heat for 10 minutes or until the celery is light brown and tender, stirring frequently. Transfer the celery to a bowl. Sprinkle with 2 teaspoons thyme and salt and mix well.

Heat 1/2 cup olive oil in a skillet until hot. Add the eggplant. Cook for 5 to 7 minutes or until light brown, stirring frequently to prevent the eggplant from burning. Stir in the tomato mixture and celery mixture. Adjust the seasonings. Simmer, covered, over low heat for 15 to 20 minutes or until of the consistency of jam, stirring frequently.

Combine the wine vinegar and sugar in a saucepan, stirring until the sugar dissolves. Stir in the vegetable mixture, olives and capers. Cook over low heat for 2 to 3 minutes or until heated through, stirring frequently. Spoon into a large serving bowl. Serve warm or at room temperature with toasted Italian bread slices.

Note: May prepare 1 to 2 days in advance and store, covered, in the refrigerator. Bring Caponata to room temperature before serving.

Portabella Pizza

SERVES 8

Pine Nut Pesto

2 cups fresh basil
$^1\!/_2$ cup pine nuts
5 garlic cloves
$^1\!/_2$ teaspoon salt
$^1\!/_2$ cup olive oil
$^2\!/_3$ cup grated Parmesan cheese

Pizza

3 to 4 tablespoons olive oil
3 tablespoons balsamic vinegar
2 teaspoons minced garlic
1 teaspoon dried thyme
8 (3- to 3$^1\!/_2$-inch) portabella mushrooms
8 slices mozzarella cheese
2 large roasted red bell peppers, peeled, sliced
2 teaspoons minced fresh oregano

For the pesto, combine the basil, pine nuts, garlic and salt in a food processor container. Process until finely minced. Add the olive oil gradually, processing constantly until smooth. Add the cheese. Process just until mixed. The leftovers may be frozen for future use.

For the pizza, preheat the oven to 350 degrees. Combine the olive oil, balsamic vinegar, garlic and thyme in a bowl and mix well. Add the mushrooms and toss to coat. Arrange the mushrooms in a single layer in a baking pan. Roast, covered, for 20 minutes or until the center is no longer white; drain.

Cut the mozzarella cheese into rounds the size of the mushrooms. Place the cheese on top of the mushrooms. Brush the cheese with $^1\!/_4$ cup of the pesto. Top with roasted red pepper slices. Bake just until the cheese melts. Sprinkle with the oregano. Arrange the mushrooms on individual plates or place on top of mixed salad greens.

The opulent surfaces of this cut-glass bowl were well suited to the formal living patterns and entertaining style of late nineteenth-century America. This extraordinary object is one of the most-visited pieces in the Museum's collection.

Libbey Glass Company
Toledo, Ohio

LIBBEY PUNCH BOWL
AND STAND
Cut glass, 1903–1904

Gift of Owens-Illinois
Glass Company

Phyllo Pizza

SERVES 10 TO 12

7 sheets phyllo pastry
^{1}/2 cup (1 stick) butter, melted
7 tablespoons grated Parmesan cheese
1 cup sliced onion
1 cup shredded mozzarella cheese
^{1}/4 cup grated Parmesan cheese
5 to 6 tomatoes, cut into ^{1}/4-inch slices
Grated Parmesan cheese to taste
1 tablespoon chopped fresh rosemary, or 1 teaspoon
   dried rosemary
^{1}/2 teaspoon dried oregano

Preheat the oven to 375 degrees. Press 1 sheet of the pastry over a buttered baking sheet with sides. Brush with some of the melted butter and sprinkle with 1 tablespoon of the 7 tablespoons Parmesan cheese. Repeat the process 6 more times with the remaining pastry, remaining butter and remaining 6 tablespoons Parmesan cheese; press.

Layer with the onion, mozzarella cheese, ^{1}/4 cup Parmesan cheese and tomatoes. Sprinkle with Parmesan cheese to taste, rosemary and oregano. Bake for 30 to 35 minutes or until brown and bubbly.

Basil and Provolone Torta

SERVES 15 TO 20

1 teaspoon extra-virgin olive oil
7 (^{1}/8-inch-thick) slices provolone cheese
12 ounces cream cheese, softened
^{1}/4 cup freshly grated Parmesan cheese
1 tablespoon minced garlic
1 tablespoon minced fresh basil
^{1}/2 teaspoon salt
^{1}/4 teaspoon freshly ground pepper
^{2}/3 cup pine nuts
12 ounces mozzarella cheese, cut into ^{1}/4-inch slices

Brush a 3-cup loaf pan with ^{1}/2 teaspoon of the olive oil. Line the pan with plastic wrap, leaving a 1-inch overlap. Brush the plastic wrap with the remaining ^{1}/2 teaspoon olive oil. Trim the provolone cheese slices to fit the pan.

Beat the cream cheese in a mixing bowl until creamy. Add the Parmesan cheese, garlic, basil, salt and pepper. Beat until mixed. Spread ^{1}/4 cup of the cheese mixture in the prepared loaf pan. Arrange 2 slices of the provolone cheese in a single layer over the cheese mixture. Spread with ^{1}/4 cup of the cheese mixture. Sprinkle with ^{1}/4 cup of the pine nuts. Spread 2 tablespoons of the cheese mixture over the pine nuts to cover.

Trim the mozzarella cheese slices to fit in a single layer in the loaf pan. Arrange half the slices in a single layer on top of the prepared layers. Spread with 2 tablespoons of the cheese mixture and arrange the remaining mozzarella cheese slices over the prepared layers. Spread with half the remaining cheese mixture. Top with the remaining 5 provolone cheese slices.

Chill, covered with plastic wrap, for 12 hours. Chill the remaining cheese mixture, covered. Bring the remaining cheese mixture to room temperature 1 hour before serving. Invert the mold onto a serving plate and remove the plastic wrap. Spread the remaining cheese mixture over the sides of the loaf. Sprinkle with the remaining pine nuts. Garnish with sprigs of Italian parsley. Serve chilled with assorted party breads or crackers.

Imperial Caviar

Homemade Mayonnaise

3 tablespoons olive oil
1 egg
1 teaspoon fresh lemon juice
1 teaspoon red wine vinegar
1 teaspoon Dijon mustard
1 teaspoon salt
Freshly ground white pepper to taste
1¹/2 cups safflower oil

Egg Layer

1 envelope unflavored gelatin
¹/4 cup cold water
4 hard-cooked eggs, chopped
¹/4 cup minced fresh parsley
1 large green onion, minced
³/4 teaspoon (or less) salt
¹/8 teaspoon hot pepper sauce
Freshly ground white pepper to taste

Avocado Layer

1 medium avocado, puréed
1 medium avocado, chopped
1 large shallot, minced
2 tablespoons lemon juice
¹/2 teaspoon salt
¹/8 teaspoon hot pepper sauce
Freshly ground pepper to taste

Sour Cream and Onion Layer

1 cup sour cream
¹/4 cup minced sweet onion

Caviar Layer

1 (3- to 4-ounce) jar black or red caviar
Fresh lemon juice to taste

For the mayonnaise, combine the olive oil, egg, lemon juice, wine vinegar, Dijon mustard, salt and white pepper in a food processor container. Process for 5 seconds. Add most of the safflower oil in a thin steady stream, processing constantly until the mayonnaise thickens. Add the remaining safflower oil more quickly. Process until blended.

For the egg layer, sprinkle the gelatin over the cold water in a saucepan. Let stand for 10 minutes. Heat over low heat until the gelatin dissolves, stirring occasionally.

Combine 1 tablespoon of the gelatin mixture, ¹/2 cup of the Homemade Mayonnaise, eggs, parsley, green onion, salt, hot pepper sauce and white pepper in a bowl and mix well. Spread in a lightly oiled 6-inch springform pan.

For the avocado layer, combine 1 tablespoon of the remaining gelatin mixture, 2 tablespoons of the Homemade Mayonnaise, avocados, shallot, lemon juice, salt, hot pepper sauce and pepper in a bowl and mix well. Spread over the prepared layer.

For the sour cream and onion layer, combine the remaining 2 tablespoons gelatin mixture, sour cream and onion in a bowl and mix well. Spread over the avocado layer. Chill, covered, in the refrigerator. May be prepared up to this point 1 day in advance and stored, covered, in the refrigerator.

For the caviar layer, rinse the caviar gently and drain. Combine with the lemon juice in a bowl and mix gently. Remove the side of the springform pan. Place the torta on a serving platter. Spread the caviar mixture over the top. Serve with cubed pumpernickel bread.

Santa Fe Cheesecake

SERVES 8 TO 10

1 cup crushed tortilla chips
3 tablespoons butter
16 ounces cream cheese, softened
2 eggs
8 ounces shredded Colby/Monterey Jack cheese blend, softened
1 (4-ounce) can chopped green chiles, drained
1/8 teaspoon hot pepper sauce
1 cup sour cream, at room temperature
1 1/2 cups salsa
1 cup chopped orange or yellow bell peppers
1/2 cup sliced scallions with tops
1/3 cup chopped tomato
1/4 cup sliced black olives

Preheat the oven to 325 degrees. Combine the tortilla chips and butter in a bowl and mix well. Press the chip mixture over the bottom of a 9-inch springform pan. Bake for 15 minutes.

Beat the cream cheese and eggs in a mixing bowl until blended, scraping the bowl occasionally. Add the shredded cheese, chiles and hot pepper sauce. Beat until mixed. Spread over the baked layer. Bake for 30 minutes longer.

Spread the sour cream over the top of the warm cheesecake. Run a sharp knife around the edge to loosen the side. Let stand until cool. Remove the side from the pan. Chill, covered, until just before serving. Spread the salsa over the top. Sprinkle with the bell peppers, scallions, tomato and olives. Serve with assorted party crackers and/or tortilla chips.

Chicken Liver Party Pâté

SERVES 10 TO 12

1 pound onions, sliced
1 pound chicken livers
1/2 cup (1 stick) butter
8 ounces cream cheese, softened
1/4 cup port
1 tablespoon Dijon mustard
1 tablespoon fresh lemon juice
2 teaspoons salt
1/4 teaspoon white pepper
1/8 teaspoon nutmeg

Sauté the onions and chicken livers in the butter in a skillet until the chicken livers are cooked through; drain. Add the cream cheese, wine, Dijon mustard, lemon juice, salt, white pepper and nutmeg. Cook until the cream cheese is melted, stirring constantly. Cool slightly.

Process the chicken liver mixture in a blender in 2 batches until puréed. Spoon into a 3- to 4-cup crock or tureen and smooth top. Chill, covered, for 4 hours. Let stand at room temperature for 30 minutes before serving. Serve with crusty French bread.

Colors of Italy

SERVES 15 TO 20

1 envelope unflavored gelatin
6 tablespoons cold water
8 ounces cream cheese, softened
4 ounces goat cheese, crumbled
1 jar pesto, drained
1 (9-ounce) jar sun-dried tomato spread
Fresh basil leaves

Line a 5- or 6-inch bowl or a loaf pan with plastic wrap. Sprinkle the gelatin over the cold water in a 2-cup microwave-safe cup. Let stand for 2 minutes. Microwave on High for 10 to 20 seconds or until the gelatin dissolves; stir. Cool to lukewarm.

Beat the cream cheese and goat cheese in a mixing bowl until blended. Stir in 2 tablespoons of the gelatin mixture.

Combine 2 tablespoons of the remaining gelatin mixture with the pesto in a bowl and mix well.

Stir the remaining 2 tablespoons of the gelatin mixture into the sun-dried tomato spread in a bowl.

Layer the pesto mixture, cream cheese mixture and sun-dried tomato mixture in the order listed in the prepared bowl or loaf pan. Chill, covered with plastic wrap, for 2 to 10 hours. Invert onto a serving platter and discard the plastic wrap. Garnish with fresh basil leaves. Serve with assorted party crackers or party breads cut into triangles.

Variation: May substitute 1 jar chopped drained oil-pack sun-dried tomatoes for the sun-dried tomato spread. May be made using a small mold as shown on page 21.

Four-Cheese Fantasy

SERVES 12 TO 18

24 ounces cream cheese
4 ounces Camembert cheese with rind, chopped
1 cup shredded Swiss cheese
4 ounces bleu cheese, crumbled
2 tablespoons sour cream
2 tablespoons milk
1 1/4 cups chopped pecans
Snipped fresh parsley
6 to 8 unpeeled apples, sliced
Lemon juice or ascorbic acid

Let the cheeses stand at room temperature for 30 minutes. Line a 9-inch tart pan, quiche pan, pie plate or cake pan with foil, plastic wrap or cheesecloth. Combine 16 ounces of the cream cheese, Camembert cheese, Swiss cheese and bleu cheese in a bowl and mix well.

Combine the remaining 8 ounces cream cheese, sour cream and milk in a bowl and stir until blended. Spread over the bottom of the prepared pan. Sprinkle with the pecans and press gently. Spread the Camembert cheese mixture over the top. Chill, covered with plastic wrap, for 2 to 3 days before serving.

Invert onto a serving platter; discard the foil. Sprinkle with parsley. Toss the apples with the lemon juice in a bowl and arrange around the cheese. Serve with the apples or assorted party crackers.

Note: Shape the cheese spread into a Christmas tree and surround with sliced Red Delicious apples during the Christmas holidays or into a heart and sprinkle with chopped red bell pepper for Valentine's Day. The flavor is enhanced if the cheese spread is allowed to chill for 1 week before serving.

The recipes featured here are, from left to right, Pretty Pepper Party Soup, Strawberry Soup, and 24 Karat Soup.

Cantaloupe Sherry Soup

SERVES 6

2 medium ripe cantaloupes, chopped
1 cup fresh orange juice
2/3 cup medium cream sherry
2/3 cup pale dry sherry
2/3 cup sour cream
4 teaspoons minced fresh spearmint leaves
6 sprigs of spearmint

Combine the cantaloupes, orange juice and sherry in a blender container. Process until puréed. Pour into a glass or plastic bowl. Stir in the sour cream and minced spearmint. Chill, covered, until serving time.

Ladle the soup into chilled glass soup bowls or demitasse cups. Top each serving with a sprig of spearmint.

Note: May prepare up to 1 day in advance and store, covered, in the refrigerator.

Strawberry Soup

MAKES 1 1/2 QUARTS

1 1/2 cups water
3/4 cup red wine
1/2 cup sugar
2 tablespoons lemon juice
1 cinnamon stick
1 quart fresh strawberries, puréed
1/2 cup whipping cream
1/4 cup sour cream

Combine the water, red wine, sugar, lemon juice and cinnamon stick in a saucepan. Bring to a boil. Boil for 15 minutes, stirring occasionally. Stir in the strawberry purée. Bring to a boil. Boil for 10 minutes longer, stirring frequently. Discard the cinnamon stick. Let stand until cool.

Beat the whipping cream in a mixing bowl until stiff peaks form. Stir in the sour cream. Fold the whipping cream mixture into the strawberry mixture. Ladle into soup bowls. Garnish each serving with a whole strawberry. Serve as a first course with a dinner of lamb and asparagus or for a ladies luncheon.

Aztec Soup

2 pounds tomatoes, peeled, chopped
1 pound boneless skinless chicken breasts, grilled, chopped
1 quart chicken stock
8 ounces green chiles, roasted, peeled, seeded, chopped
1/2 green bell pepper, chopped
1/2 large onion, chopped
1/2 bunch (1/4 to 1/3 cup) cilantro, chopped
2 tablespoons lime juice
1/2 teaspoon cumin
1/4 teaspoon black pepper
2 cups crumbled tortilla chips
1 cup (or more) shredded Monterey Jack cheese

Combine the tomatoes, chicken, stock, chiles, bell pepper, onion, cilantro, lime juice, cumin and black pepper in a stockpot and mix well. Bring to a simmer. Simmer for 20 minutes, stirring occasionally.

Divide the tortilla chips and cheese evenly among 6 soup bowls. Ladle the soup over the chips and cheese. Sprinkle with additional cheese if desired. Serve immediately.

Note: May substitute pork or beef for the chicken or add chopped jalapeño chiles. May prepare several days in advance before addition of chips and cheese, and store, covered, in the refrigerator. Reheat before serving.

Potage Argenteuil

1 pound fresh asparagus, trimmed
3 tablespoons butter
2 leeks, trimmed, chopped
1 1/2 cups chopped peeled potatoes
4 1/2 cups chicken or vegetable stock
6 tablespoons light cream
2 tablespoons chopped fresh chives
1/8 teaspoon freshly grated nutmeg
Salt and pepper to taste

Chop the asparagus, reserving the tips. Heat the butter in a large saucepan until melted. Add the chopped asparagus, leeks and potatoes. Sauté for 5 minutes. Stir in the stock. Bring to a boil; reduce heat.

Simmer, covered, for 20 minutes, stirring occasionally. Pour into a blender or food processor container. Process until smooth. Pour the soup into a clean saucepan. Stir in the light cream, chives and nutmeg. Season with salt and pepper. Heat just until warm, stirring occasionally. Remove from heat. Cover to keep warm.

Blanch the reserved asparagus tips in boiling water in a saucepan for 2 minutes or until tender crisp. Drain and immerse in cold water. Drain and pat dry. Ladle the soup into heated soup bowls. Top each serving with some of the asparagus tips. Garnish with additional chopped fresh chives.

Note: May prepare 2 to 3 days in advance and store, covered, in the refrigerator. Reheat before serving.

A shallow oval bowl for soup rests on two recumbent figures of goats or hinds (female red deer). Its sides are festooned with flowers, foliage, and a band of shallow flutes, while the cover is decorated with apples, cherries, and leaves.

Paul Crespin
English, 1694–1770

TUREEN WITH STAND AND LINER
Silver, 1740

Purchased with funds from the Florence Scott Libbey Bequest, in Memory of her Father, Maurice A. Scott

Escarole and White Bean Soup

SERVES 8

4 ounces lean ground beef
4 ounces ground pork
1 egg, beaten
2 tablespoons freshly grated Parmesan cheese
2 tablespoons seasoned dry bread crumbs
$^1/_4$ teaspoon garlic powder
8 cups chicken broth
2 (16-ounce) cans cannellini, drained
1 large bunch escarole, chopped
1 garlic clove, minced
$^1/_2$ teaspoon red pepper flakes
$^1/_2$ teaspoon basil, crushed
Salt and freshly ground black pepper to taste

Combine the ground beef, ground pork, egg, cheese, bread crumbs and garlic powder in a bowl and mix well. Shape into 1-inch balls.

Heat the broth in a large saucepan over medium heat. Stir in the beans, escarole, minced garlic, red pepper flakes, basil, salt and black pepper. Add the meatballs and mix gently. Cook for 30 minutes or until the meatballs are cooked through, stirring occasionally. Ladle into soup bowls. Serve immediately with additional Parmesan cheese.

Note: May prepare up to 1 day in advance and store, covered, in the refrigerator. Reheat before serving.

La Jolla Smoked Chicken and Black Bean Soup

SERVES 4

1 cup chopped peeled broccoli stems
1/2 cup each chopped carrots, onion and celery
1/4 cup (1/2 stick) unsalted butter
2 teaspoons each dried thyme and oregano
1 teaspoon dried basil
1/4 cup dry white wine
4 cups chicken stock, heated
1 cup chopped smoked chicken
1 cup cooked black beans
1 cup fresh broccoli florets
1 tablespoon Worcestershire sauce
1/2 teaspoon Tabasco sauce
2 cups half-and-half
Salt and freshly ground pepper to taste
2 tablespoons cornstarch (optional)
1/4 cup (1/2 stick) unsalted butter, chopped

Sauté the broccoli stems, carrots, onion and celery in 1/4 cup butter in a saucepan for 5 minutes. Stir in the thyme, oregano and basil. Sauté for 5 minutes. Deglaze with the white wine. Stir in the stock. Cook until reduced by 1/3, stirring frequently.

Add the smoked chicken, beans, broccoli florets, Worcestershire sauce and Tabasco sauce and mix well. Simmer for 5 minutes, stirring occasionally. Stir in the half-and-half. Simmer for 5 minutes longer, stirring occasionally. Season with salt and pepper.

Combine the cornstarch with just enough water in a bowl to form a paste if needed to thicken. Stir into the soup. Add 1/4 cup butter gradually, stirring constantly. Cook just until the butter melts, stirring constantly. Ladle into soup bowls. Serve immediately.

Note: To prepare the smoked chicken, smoke boneless chicken breasts in a covered grill for 30 minutes or until medium-rare. Add apple chips to the coals for a wonderful flavor.

24 Karat Soup

SERVES 4

1/2 medium onion, chopped
2 ribs celery, chopped
1 small leek, chopped
1 1/2 tablespoons butter
1 tablespoon flour
4 cups chicken stock
1 pound fresh carrots, sliced
1/8 teaspoon nutmeg
Salt and white pepper to taste
1/2 cup heavy cream
1/2 cup milk

Sauté the onion, celery and leek in the butter in a saucepan until tender. Sprinkle with the flour. Add the stock gradually, stirring constantly. Bring to a boil; reduce heat. Simmer for 15 minutes, stirring occasionally.

Add the carrots, nutmeg, salt and white pepper and mix well. Simmer for 20 minutes or until the carrots are tender, stirring occasionally. Pour the soup mixture into a blender container. Process until puréed. Return the purée to the saucepan. Stir in the heavy cream and milk.

Cook just until heated through, stirring frequently; do not boil. Ladle into small pumpkins that have been hollowed out to form bowls. Garnish with yellow bell pepper stars and fresh chives.

Note: May prepare up to 1 day in advance and store, covered, in the refrigerator. Reheat before serving.

Lemon Chicken Soup

SERVES 6

1 large onion, chopped
2 large garlic cloves, chopped
2 tablespoons olive oil
1 large red bell pepper, chopped
3 ribs celery, chopped
2 carrots, chopped
8 cups (or more) chicken broth
2 cups cooked bow tie pasta (cooked al dente)
2 cups chopped cooked chicken
2 tablespoons fresh lemon juice
2 tablespoons grated lemon zest
1/2 (10-ounce) package fresh spinach
Salt and pepper to taste
Grated Parmesan cheese (optional)

Sauté the onion and garlic in the olive oil in a large saucepan over medium heat for 1 minute. Add the bell pepper, celery and carrots. Sauté for 8 minutes or until the vegetables are tender. Stir in the broth. Bring to a boil; reduce heat to medium-low.

Add the pasta, chicken, lemon juice and lemon zest to the broth mixture and mix well. Stir in the spinach. Cook for 3 to 5 minutes, stirring occasionally. Season with salt and pepper. Ladle into soup bowls. Sprinkle with the cheese.

Note: Add additional broth if needed for a thinner consistency. May be frozen for future use.

Corn and Cheddar Chowder

SERVES 4

1 (10-ounce) package frozen Shoe Peg corn
2 cups water
Salt to taste
1 large potato, peeled, chopped
1 bay leaf
1/2 teaspoon cumin
1/4 teaspoon dried sage
1 onion, finely chopped
3 tablespoons butter
3 tablespoons flour
1 1/4 cups heavy cream or half-and-half
Pepper to taste
2 cups shredded sharp Cheddar cheese
1/2 cup dry white wine

Cook the corn using package directions; drain. Bring the water and salt to a boil in a saucepan. Add the potato, bay leaf, cumin and sage. Return to a boil. Boil for 20 minutes or until the potato is tender.

Sauté the onion in the butter in a saucepan until tender. Stir in the flour. Whisk in the heavy cream. Stir into the potato mixture. Add the corn and mix well. Season with salt and pepper. Simmer for 10 minutes, stirring occasionally. Stir in the cheese and white wine.

Simmer just until the cheese melts, stirring frequently. Discard the bay leaf. Ladle into soup bowls. Garnish each serving with sprigs of parsley and chopped fresh chives.

Note: May prepare in advance and store, covered, in the refrigerator, adding the cheese and wine just before serving.

scarole and White Bean Soup—
Simple rustic fare

Chilled Cucumber Soup

SERVES 8

3 cups chicken broth
3 medium cucumbers, peeled, seeded, chopped
2 cups sour cream
3 tablespoons white vinegar
2 teaspoons salt
2 garlic cloves

Combine the broth, cucumbers, sour cream, vinegar, salt and garlic in a food processor container. Process until smooth. Transfer to a bowl. Chill, covered, until serving time or for up to 1 day in advance. Ladle into soup bowls. Garnish with sprigs of dillweed or fresh chives.

Crème Vichyssoise

SERVES 6 TO 8

6 leek bulbs, finely chopped
2 medium onions, finely chopped
1/2 cup (1 stick) butter
2 quarts chicken stock
12 ounces white potatoes, peeled, finely chopped
Salt and white pepper to taste
1 cup cream
Finely chopped fresh chives

Cook the leeks and onions in the butter in a large saucepan over low heat until tender, stirring frequently; do not brown. Stir in the stock and potatoes. Season with salt and white pepper. Cook until the potatoes are tender, stirring occasionally. Press the potato mixture through a fine strainer into a bowl. Stir in the cream. Chill, covered, until serving time. Ladle into soup bowls. Sprinkle with chives.

Shrimp Gazpacho

SERVES 8

1 (32-ounce) bottle clamato juice
2 tablespoons olive oil
2 tablespoons red wine vinegar
2 tablespoons fresh lemon juice
1 tablespoon sugar
1 garlic clove, crushed
1/2 teaspoon (or more) Tabasco sauce
1 pound cooked shrimp, peeled, deveined, cut into
   bite-size pieces
2 large tomatoes, minced
1/2 cup finely chopped peeled cucumber
1/3 cup thinly sliced green onions
1 avocado, sliced
4 ounces cream cheese, cubed
Chopped fresh cilantro (optional)

Combine the clamato juice, olive oil, wine vinegar, lemon juice, sugar, garlic and Tabasco sauce in a glass bowl and mix well. Stir in the shrimp, tomatoes, cucumber and green onions. Chill, covered, for 2 to 10 hours. Ladle into chilled soup bowls. Top each serving with an avocado slice, several cream cheese cubes and cilantro.

Note: The flavor of the soup is enhanced if chilled overnight.

Maumee Mushroom Soup

MAKES 2 QUARTS

1 quart chicken broth
1 pound fresh mushrooms, finely chopped
1 medium onion, chopped
6 tablespoons (3/4 stick) butter
6 tablespoons flour
1 teaspoon salt
1 teaspoon white pepper
1 teaspoon minced garlic
1/8 teaspoon Tabasco sauce
2 tablespoons sherry
2 1/2 to 3 cups milk

Reserve 1/2 cup of the broth. Combine the remaining broth, mushrooms and onion in a saucepan. Simmer until the vegetables are tender, stirring occasionally. Heat the butter in a saucepan until melted. Add the flour, whisking until blended. Stir in the salt, white pepper, garlic and Tabasco sauce. Cook until bubbly, stirring constantly. Add the reserved broth and mix well. Stir in the mushroom mixture and sherry. The mixture may be frozen at this point for future use.

Cook until of the desired consistency, stirring frequently. Add the milk until of the desired consistency, stirring constantly. Cook just until heated through. Ladle into soup bowls. Serve immediately.

Note: May prepare several days in advance and store, covered, in the refrigerator. Reheat before serving.

Spring Soup

SERVES 6

2 (10-ounce) packages frozen chopped spinach, thawed, drained
1 large onion, chopped
1/2 cup (1 stick) butter
5 cups chicken stock
2 (10-ounce) packages frozen peas
1 tablespoon crushed chopped fresh mint
1 1/2 cups half-and-half
1 teaspoon salt, or to taste
1/2 teaspoon pepper, or to taste

Press the spinach to remove the excess moisture. Sauté the onion in the butter in a saucepan until tender. Stir in the spinach. Add the stock, peas and mint and mix well. Simmer for 20 minutes, stirring occasionally.

Transfer the soup to a food processor container. Process until puréed. Return the soup to the saucepan. Stir in the half-and-half, salt and pepper. Cook just until heated through; do not boil. Ladle into soup bowls. Garnish with sprigs of fresh mint. Serve immediately.

Note: May prepare 1 to 2 days in advance and store, covered, in the refrigerator. Reheat before serving or serve chilled. The soup may be frozen for future use, adding the half-and-half just before serving.

Pretty Pepper Party Soup

SERVES 4

2 tablespoons butter
2 medium carrots, chopped
1 large onion, chopped
1¼ cups chicken broth
1 yellow bell pepper, chopped
3 ounces cream cheese, chopped, softened
½ teaspoon salt
⅛ teaspoon cayenne pepper
⅛ teaspoon nutmeg
½ cup light cream

Heat the butter in a saucepan until melted. Add the carrots and onion and mix well. Cook for 10 minutes or until the vegetables are tender, stirring frequently. Stir in the broth and bell pepper.

Simmer until the bell pepper is tender, stirring occasionally. Cool slightly. Stir in the cream cheese, salt, cayenne pepper and nutmeg. Add the light cream and mix well. Let stand until cool.

Transfer the soup to a blender or food processor container. Process until smooth. Return the soup to the saucepan. Cook just until heated through, stirring frequently; do not boil. Ladle into soup bowls, cups or mugs. Garnish each serving with carrot crescents and Italian parsley.

Potato Carrot Soup

SERVES 4 TO 6

12 ounces sweet potatoes
8 ounces baking potatoes
1¾ pounds unpeeled carrots, sliced
6 ounces onions, coarsely chopped
5 cups rich chicken stock
1 tablespoon fresh lemon juice
1 teaspoon salt
½ teaspoon freshly ground white pepper
2 tablespoons (heaping) finely chopped fresh dillweed
Sour cream

Preheat the oven to 400 degrees. Arrange the sweet potatoes and baking potatoes on a nonstick baking sheet. Bake for 1 hour or until tender. Steam the carrots until tender; drain. Place the carrots in a food processor container.

Sauté the onions in a skillet sprayed with nonstick cooking spray until light golden brown. Spoon the sautéed onions into the food processor container. Deglaze the skillet with some of the stock. Add to the food processor. Process until puréed.

Peel the sweet potatoes and baking potatoes and chop the pulp. Add the pulp, lemon juice, salt and white pepper to the purée. Process until mixed and smooth. Transfer the soup to a saucepan. Stir in the remaining stock and dillweed. Simmer for 15 minutes, stirring frequently. Ladle into soup bowls. Top each serving with a dollop of sour cream.

Note: Add additional stock to the soup for a thinner consistency.

Curried Butternut Squash Soup

SERVES 8

2 tablespoons butter
2 large carrots, peeled, sliced
1 cup chopped yellow onion
1 garlic clove, minced
1 tablespoon minced gingerroot
2 teaspoons curry powder
^{1}/4 teaspoon cinnamon
^{1}/8 teaspoon nutmeg
2 (2-pound) butternut squash, peeled, seeded, chopped
3 cups (or more) apple juice
^{1}/4 cup heavy cream

Heat the butter in a saucepan over medium-high heat until melted. Add the carrots, onion and garlic and mix well. Sauté for 5 minutes or until the vegetables are tender. Stir in the gingerroot, curry powder, cinnamon and nutmeg. Cook for 1 minute. Stir in the squash and apple juice. Bring to a boil; reduce heat.

Simmer, covered, for 30 minutes or until the squash is tender. Process the soup in batches in a food processor or blender until smooth. Return the soup to the saucepan, adding additional apple juice if needed for the desired consistency. Stir in the heavy cream. Cook just until heated through, stirring occasionally. Ladle into soup bowls. Drizzle with additional whipping cream. Serve immediately with crackers.

Note: May prepare up to 1 day in advance and store, covered, in the refrigerator. Reheat before serving.

A marine fantasy of realistically modelled large and small shells, fish, crabs, barnacles and other sea encrustations decorate this ladle—and would have impressed dinner guests at elegant parties typical of the late nineteenth-century American elite.

Gorham Manufacturing Company American

LADLE
Silver partly gilded, about 1880

Purchased with funds from The Florence Scott Libbey Bequest, in Memory of her Father, Maurice A. Scott

Tomato Basil Soup

SERVES 6

1 vegetable or chicken bouillon cube
2 cups hot water
1 bunch scallions, chopped
1 onion, chopped
1 red bell pepper, chopped
1 tablespoon olive oil
1 (28-ounce) can tomatoes
Juice of 1 orange
1 large garlic clove, crushed
1 tablespoon (heaping) tomato paste
1 teaspoon (heaping) brown sugar
$1/2$ teaspoon salt
15 grinds of pepper
2 bay leaves
$1/2$ cup (about) fresh basil leaves

Dissolve the bouillon cube in the hot water in a bowl. Sauté the scallions, onion and bell pepper in the olive oil in a saucepan until tender and golden; do not brown. Stir in the bouillon, undrained tomatoes, orange juice, garlic, tomato paste, brown sugar, salt, pepper and bay leaves.

Simmer, covered, for 30 minutes, stirring occasionally. Discard the bay leaves. Process the soup in a blender or food processor until puréed. Return all but 1 cup of the soup to the saucepan. Process the basil with 1 cup soup until the basil is finely chopped. Stir into the soup. Cook just until heated through, stirring frequently. Ladle into soup bowls. Garnish with additional fresh basil, fresh chives and croutons.

Note: The flavor is enhanced if the soup is allowed to stand, covered, in the refrigerator for 2 to 10 hours. Reheat the soup before serving.

Minestrone with Sweet Sausage

SERVES 8

8 ounces sweet Italian sausage, sliced
2 tablespoons olive oil
1 cup chopped onion
1 cup chopped carrots
1 garlic clove, minced
1 teaspoon basil
2 (10-ounce) cans beef consommé
2 consommé cans water
1 (16-ounce) can Italian tomatoes
2 small zucchini, sliced
2 cups finely shredded cabbage
Salt and pepper to taste
1 (16-ounce) can Great Northern beans
$1/2$ cup rice
$1/2$ cup red wine

Brown the sausage in the olive oil in a saucepan; drain. Add the onion, carrots, garlic and basil. Cook for 5 minutes, stirring frequently. Stir in the consommé, water, undrained tomatoes, zucchini, cabbage, salt and pepper.

Simmer for 1 hour, stirring occasionally. Add the undrained beans, rice and red wine and mix well. Cook for 20 minutes or until the rice is tender, stirring occasionally. Ladle into soup bowls. Garnish each serving with chopped fresh parsley and freshly grated Parmesan cheese. Serve with French bread.

Note: May prepare several days in advance and store, covered, in the refrigerator. Reheat before serving.

Jarlsberg Vegetable Soup

SERVES 6 TO 8

1/4 cup (1/2 stick) butter
3 tablespoons flour
4 cups chicken broth
2 cups coarsely chopped broccoli
3/4 cup chopped carrots
1/2 cup chopped celery
1 medium onion, chopped
2 garlic cloves, minced
1/2 teaspoon salt
1/4 teaspoon thyme
1/8 teaspoon pepper
1 cup heavy cream
1 egg yolk
1 1/2 cups shredded Jarlsberg cheese

Heat the butter in a saucepan until melted. Add the flour, stirring until blended. Cook for several minutes or until bubbly, stirring constantly. Remove from heat. Add the broth gradually, stirring constantly. Stir in the broccoli, carrots, celery, onion, garlic, salt, thyme and pepper.

Simmer, covered, for 8 to 10 minutes or until the vegetables are tender, stirring occasionally. Whisk the heavy cream and egg yolk in a bowl until blended. Stir several tablespoons of the hot mixture into the cream mixture. Add the cream mixture to the hot mixture. Cook until thickened, stirring constantly. Stir in the cheese. Ladle into soup bowls.

Note: The secret of this recipe is constant stirring and not allowing the soup to come to a boil. May prepare 1 to 2 days in advance and store, covered, in the refrigerator. Reheat before serving.

Red Hot Chili

SERVES 8 TO 10

2 pounds coarsely ground round steak
1/4 cup bacon drippings
2 pounds round steak, cut into 1/2-inch cubes
1 large onion, chopped
4 garlic cloves, crushed
1 (48-ounce) can beef broth
1 (15-ounce) can tomato sauce
1 (12-ounce) bottle beer
2 (4-ounce) cans chopped green chiles, drained
1/4 cup chili powder
1 to 2 tablespoons crushed red pepper, or to taste
1 tablespoon each cumin, oregano, cumin seeds, paprika, sugar
   and salt
1 teaspoon black pepper
1 teaspoon Tabasco sauce

Brown the ground round in 2 tablespoons of the bacon drippings in a skillet, stirring until crumbly. Drain, reserving the pan drippings. Brown the round steak in the remaining 2 tablespoons bacon drippings in a separate skillet. Drain, reserving the pan drippings. Heat the reserved drippings in a skillet until hot. Add the onion and garlic. Sauté until the onion is tender.

Combine the ground round, round steak, onion mixture, broth, tomato sauce, beer, chiles, chili powder, red pepper, cumin, oregano, cumin seeds, paprika, sugar, salt, black pepper and Tabasco sauce in a large saucepan and mix well. Simmer for 2 hours or until of the desired consistency, stirring occasionally. Ladle into chili bowls. The flavor is enhanced if the chili is chilled and reheated before serving.

Variation: This is a traditional Texas-style chili, comprised mainly of beef and without beans or tomatoes as ingredients. May add one 14-ounce can diced tomatoes before simmering and two 15-ounce cans drained beans just before serving.

Venison Chili

SERVES 6

1/4 cup unsalted butter
1 red onion, chopped
4 garlic cloves, minced
1/4 cup packed dark brown sugar
4 cups chicken stock
3 cups red wine
1/4 cup each red wine vinegar and tomato paste
2 tablespoons finely chopped fresh cilantro
1 teaspoon cumin
1/2 teaspoon each cayenne pepper and chili powder
Salt to taste
1/4 cup canola oil
1 cup chopped bacon
2 pounds venison stew meat, trimmed, finely chopped
2 cups cooked black beans

Heat the butter in a stockpot over medium heat until melted. Add the onion and garlic. Sauté for 3 to 4 minutes or until the onion is tender. Stir in the brown sugar. Cook for 2 to 3 minutes or until the onion and garlic are light brown. Add the stock, red wine, wine vinegar, tomato paste, cilantro, cumin, cayenne pepper, chili powder and salt and mix well. Bring to a simmer, stirring occasionally. Simmer for 30 to 35 minutes or until reduced by 1/2.

Heat the canola oil in a skillet over high heat. Fry the bacon in the hot oil for 2 to 3 minutes or until brown. Push the bacon to the side of the skillet. Add the venison. Season with salt. Cook for 20 minutes or until the venison is brown on all sides and most of the liquid has evaporated, stirring frequently. Stir in the black beans. Stir the venison mixture into the sauce.

Bring the chili to a simmer. Simmer for 20 minutes or until thickened, stirring occasionally. Adjust the seasonings. Ladle into chili bowls. Serve with corn bread or flat bread.

Note: May prepare 1 to 2 days in advance and store, covered, in the refrigerator. Reheat before serving.

Shrimp Gumbo

SERVES 6 TO 8

1 cup chopped onion
1/2 cup chopped fresh parsley
1/2 cup chopped celery
4 green onions, chopped with half the tops
1 garlic clove, crushed
3 tablespoons vegetable oil
3 tablespoons corn oil
3 tablespoons flour
2 quarts water
2 tablespoons red wine
1 teaspoon Worcestershire sauce
1/2 teaspoon sugar
2 pounds peeled shrimp
1/2 cup chopped green bell pepper or sliced okra
1 teaspoon filé powder
3 cups cooked rice

Sauté the onion, parsley, celery, green onions and garlic in the vegetable oil in a skillet until the vegetables are tender. Heat the corn oil in a saucepan until hot. Add the flour, stirring constantly until blended. Cook over medium to low heat until the flour is golden brown, stirring constantly. Stir in the vegetable mixture. Add the water, red wine, Worcestershire sauce and sugar and mix well.

Cook over medium to low heat for 1 hour, stirring occasionally. Stir in the shrimp and bell pepper. Simmer for 15 minutes or until the shrimp turn pink, stirring occasionally. Stir in the filé powder. Ladle over the rice in soup bowls.

Note: May prepare up to 1 day in advance and store, covered, in the refrigerator. Reheat before serving.

Savory Seafood Stew

SERVES 6

2 garlic cloves, minced
2 tablespoons olive oil
1 cup chopped onion
1 cup chopped green bell pepper
3 ribs celery, chopped
1 (28-ounce) can chopped tomatoes
1 cup water
1/2 cup white wine
1 tablespoon Italian seasoning
4 ounces red snapper, cut into bite-size pieces
12 ounces mahimahi, cut into bite-size pieces
12 ounces halibut, cut into bite-size pieces
Freshly ground Romano cheese (optional)

Sauté the garlic in the olive oil in a stockpot until light brown. Stir in the onion, bell pepper and celery. Sauté until the onion is tender. Add the undrained tomatoes, water, white wine and Italian seasoning and mix well.

Simmer for 30 minutes, stirring occasionally. Stir in the red snapper, mahimahi and halibut. Simmer for 15 minutes longer or until the fish is cooked through, stirring occasionally. Ladle into soup bowls. Sprinkle with Romano cheese.

Note: Store leftovers in the refrigerator. The stew is just as good the next day.

Variations: May substitute 3 1/2 cups chopped seeded peeled fresh tomatoes for the canned tomatoes. The total weight of the fish is 1 3/4 pounds and may be varied to taste and availability. Steak-texture fish works best as it does not tend to fall apart while cooking. Shellfish, such as scallops and shrimp, also work well. This is a stew, so mistakes are hard to make.

Vegetarian Sierra Stew

SERVES 6

1 cup dried kidney beans
1 large onion, thinly sliced, cut into quarters
4 large garlic cloves, minced
2 tablespoons olive oil
1 (14-ounce) can whole tomatoes, cut into quarters
1 green bell pepper, coarsely chopped
1 cup coarsely chopped green cabbage
1/2 cup chopped unpeeled russet potato
1 tablespoon chili powder, or to taste
1/2 teaspoon cumin
4 cups water or vegetable broth
1/2 cup uncooked brown rice
Herbal salt and freshly ground pepper to taste
1/4 cup shredded jalapeño or pepper Monterey Jack cheese
   (optional)

Sort and rinse the beans. Combine the beans with enough cold water to cover in a bowl. Let stand for 8 to 10 hours. Drain and rinse the beans. Sauté the onion and garlic in the olive oil in a stockpot over medium heat for 3 to 5 minutes or until the onion is tender. Stir in the undrained tomatoes, bell pepper, cabbage, potato, chili powder and cumin.

Cook for 3 minutes, stirring occasionally. Stir in the beans, water and brown rice. Cook, covered, over low heat for 2 hours or until the beans are tender and the stew is thickened, stirring occasionally. Season with herbal salt and pepper. Ladle into soups bowls. Sprinkle with the cheese. Top with salsa and sour cream if desired. Serve with corn bread muffins.

Note: May prepare up to 1 day in advance and store, covered, in the refrigerator. Reheat before serving.

The recipe featured here is Pear, Walnut and Bleu Cheese Salad.

Bloody Mary Aspic

SERVES 8

1 envelope unflavored gelatin
1¹/2 cups tomato juice
1 (6-ounce) package lemon gelatin
1¹/3 cups Bloody Mary mix
2 tablespoons Worcestershire sauce
1 teaspoon celery salt
1 teaspoon cider vinegar
1 teaspoon dry mustard
Tabasco sauce to taste
2 (6-ounce) packages frozen shrimp, thawed,
    drained, chopped
1 cup chopped celery
1 cup chopped cucumber

Soften the unflavored gelatin in 2 tablespoons of the tomato juice in a small bowl. Bring the remaining tomato juice to a boil in a saucepan. Add the unflavored gelatin mixture and lemon gelatin and mix well. Stir in the Bloody Mary mix. Add the Worcestershire sauce, celery salt, vinegar, dry mustard and Tabasco sauce and mix well.

Stir the shrimp, celery and cucumber into the gelatin mixture. Pour into an 8-cup mold. Chill, covered, until set. Invert onto a serving platter lined with lettuce. Serve immediately.

Variation: Add 1 additional envelope unflavored gelatin for an extra-firm aspic. This is a classic for brunch.

Tossed Apple Salad

SERVES 8 TO 10

Poppy Seed Dressing
1 cup salad oil
¹/4 cup sugar
¹/3 cup wine vinegar
1 tablespoon poppy seeds
Salad
1 head Boston lettuce, torn
1 package fresh spinach, trimmed, torn
8 unpeeled apples, cut into bite-size pieces (use combination of
    red, yellow and green)
1 pound Swiss cheese, cut into bite-size pieces
1 cup dry-roasted cashews

For the dressing, combine the salad oil, sugar, wine vinegar and poppy seeds in a jar with a tight-fitting lid. Cover and shake to mix. Store in the refrigerator.

For the salad, toss the lettuce, spinach, apples, cheese and cashews in a salad bowl. Add the dressing and mix well. Serve immediately.

Note: To keep the apples from turning brown, toss with lemon, orange or grapefruit juice.

Lake Erie Cherry Salad

SERVES 8

Sesame Dressing
$1/2$ cup salad oil
$1/2$ cup sugar
$1/4$ cup cider vinegar
2 tablespoons sesame seeds
$1^1/2$ teaspoons minced onion
$1/4$ teaspoon paprika
$1/4$ teaspoon Worcestershire sauce
Salt and pepper to taste
Salad
Bibb lettuce, torn into bite-size pieces
Leaf lettuce, torn into bite-size pieces
Romaine, torn into bite-size pieces
1 (11-ounce) can mandarin oranges, drained
$1/2$ cup dried cherries
$1/2$ cup sliced almonds, toasted

For the dressing, combine the salad oil, sugar, vinegar, sesame seeds, onion, paprika, Worcestershire sauce, salt and pepper in a blender container. Process until smooth. Chill, covered, until serving time.

For the salad, toss the Bibb lettuce, leaf lettuce and romaine in a salad bowl. Add the oranges, cherries and almonds and mix gently. Add the dressing and toss gently to coat.

Note: May substitute $1/2$ cup dried cranberries for the cherries.

Sherry Cherry

SERVES 6 TO 8

1 large can pitted sweet cherries
$1/2$ cup sherry
2 (3-ounce) packages cherry gelatin
3 ounces cream cheese, softened
1 cup pecans

Drain the cherries, reserving the juice. Combine the reserved juice and wine with enough water to measure 3 cups. Pour into a saucepan. Bring to a boil. Add the gelatin, stirring until dissolved. Chill until partially set.

Stuff each cherry with some of the cream cheese. Stir the cherries and pecans into the gelatin. Spoon into a 2-quart ring mold. Chill until set. Invert onto a lettuce-lined serving platter.

Cranberry Waldorf Salad

SERVES 8

2 cups fresh cranberries, ground
$1/3$ cup honey
2 cups chopped unpeeled tart apples
1 cup seedless green grape halves
$1/2$ cup chopped English walnuts
$1/4$ teaspoon salt
1 cup heavy cream

Combine the cranberries with the honey in a bowl and mix well. Chill, covered, for 8 hours. Stir in the apples, grapes, walnuts and salt. Whip the cream in a mixing bowl until soft peaks form. Fold the whipped cream into the salad. Chill, covered, for several hours. Garnish with green grape clusters and whole fresh cranberries.

T

he arrangement of fruit, nuts, and a full wineglass expresses abundance, albeit sensibly moderated in a typically American way. The spiraling orange peel suggests a visual pun on the artist's name.

Raphaelle Peale
American, 1774–1825

STILL LIFE WITH ORANGES
Oil on wood panel, about 1818

Purchased with funds from the Florence Scott Libbey Bequest, in Memory of her Father, Maurice A. Scott

Frozen Cranberry Gingersnap Salad

SERVES 8

2 cups crushed gingersnap cookies
$1/4$ cup ($1/2$ stick) butter, melted
8 ounces cream cheese, softened
1 (16-ounce) can whole berry cranberry sauce
1 cup sour cream
1 tablespoon brown sugar
$1/2$ cup sour cream

Combine the cookie crumbs and butter in a bowl and mix well. Reserve $1/3$ cup of the crumb mixture. Press the remaining crumb mixture over the bottom of a greased 8×8-inch dish.

Beat the cream cheese in a mixing bowl at medium speed until smooth. Stir in the cranberry sauce, 1 cup sour cream and brown sugar. Spoon into the prepared dish.

Freeze, covered, until set. Let stand at room temperature for 20 minutes before cutting into squares.

Top each serving with 1 tablespoon of the $1/2$ cup sour cream. Sprinkle with the reserved crumb mixture.

Note: May prepare up to 1 week in advance and store, covered, in the freezer. Great served during the holidays with turkey and chicken.

Praline Orange Salad

SERVES 8 TO 10

Picante Dressing
1/2 cup vegetable oil
1/4 cup vinegar
1/4 cup sugar
2 tablespoons chopped fresh parsley
1/2 teaspoon salt
5 to 10 drops of Tabasco sauce
1/8 teaspoon pepper
Salad
1/2 cup sliced almonds
2 1/2 tablespoons sugar
1 head lettuce, torn into bite-size pieces
1 pound romaine, torn into bite-size pieces
3 ribs celery, chopped
4 green onions, thinly sliced
Sliced fresh oranges, clementines, or 1 (16-ounce) can
*   mandarin oranges, drained (optional)*

For the dressing, combine the oil, vinegar, sugar, parsley, salt, Tabasco sauce and pepper in a jar with a tight-fitting lid. Cover the jar and shake to mix.

For the salad, combine the almonds and sugar in a skillet. Cook over low heat until the sugar melts and the almonds are coated, stirring constantly. Spread the almonds on waxed paper. Let stand until cool. Break into pieces.

Toss the lettuce, romaine, celery and green onions in a salad bowl. Add the oranges and dressing just before serving and mix well. Sprinkle with the almonds.

Jicama, Mango and Watercress Salad

SERVES 8

Cilantro Vinaigrette
3/4 cup walnut oil or olive oil
6 tablespoons white wine vinegar
5 tablespoons chopped fresh cilantro
3 tablespoons chopped pecans, toasted
Salt and pepper to taste
Salad
2 large bunches watercress, trimmed
2 cups julienned peeled jicama
2 cups julienned mango
2 small red bell peppers, julienned
Salt and pepper to taste
1/2 cup pecan halves, toasted

For the vinaigrette, whisk the walnut oil, wine vinegar and cilantro in a bowl. Stir in the pecans. Season with salt and pepper. You may prepare up to 2 hours in advance.

For the salad, combine the watercress, jicama, mango and bell peppers in a large salad bowl. Add just enough of the vinaigrette to coat and mix well. Season with salt and pepper. Divide the salad evenly among 8 salad plates. Sprinkle with the pecans. Serve immediately.

Variation: May substitute different varieties of greens for the watercress, such as romaine or iceberg lettuce.

Pear, Walnut and Bleu Cheese Salad

SERVES 6

Shallot Dressing
$1/2$ cup salad oil
2 tablespoons fresh lemon juice
1 large shallot, minced
$1/2$ teaspoon sugar
$1/2$ teaspoon pepper
Salad
4 cups lightly packed arugula
4 cups torn butter lettuce
2 small ripe firm pears, thinly sliced
$1/2$ cup walnut pieces, toasted
$1/2$ cup dried cherries (optional)
$1/2$ cup crumbled bleu cheese
Salt to taste

For the dressing, whisk the salad oil, lemon juice, shallot, sugar and pepper in a bowl.

For the salad, toss the arugula, butter lettuce, pears, walnuts and cherries in a large salad bowl. Add just enough dressing to coat and mix gently. Divide the salad equally among 6 salad plates. Sprinkle with the cheese and salt.

Chinese Chicken Salad

SERVES 6

Sesame Dressing
$1/2$ cup cider vinegar
$1/2$ cup vegetable oil
$1/2$ cup sugar
$1/4$ cup sesame oil
$1/4$ cup sesame seeds, toasted
1 each teaspoon salt and pepper
Salad
6 boneless skinless chicken breast halves
1 cup orange juice
$1/2$ cup honey
1 tablespoon Dijon mustard
2 teaspoons lemon pepper
$3/4$ teaspoon ginger powder
1 garlic clove, crushed
1 head romaine, torn into bite-size pieces
1 cup bamboo shoots
1 cup pea pods
1 cup cashews
$1/2$ cup chopped green onions
2 (11-ounce) cans mandarin oranges, drained

For the dressing, combine the first 7 ingredients in a jar with a tight-fitting lid. Shake to mix.

For the salad, arrange the chicken in a single layer in a shallow dish. Whisk the orange juice, honey, Dijon mustard, lemon pepper, ginger and garlic in a bowl. Pour over the chicken, turning to coat. Marinate, covered, in the refrigerator for 2 to 3 hours, turning occasionally; drain. Grill the chicken over hot coals or broil until cooked through. Cool slightly. Cut into thin slices.

Toss the romaine, bamboo shoots, pea pods, cashews and green onions in a bowl. Arrange the romaine mixture evenly on each of 6 serving plates. Top each serving with 1 sliced chicken breast and some of the mandarin oranges. Drizzle with the dressing.

B*lack-Eyed Pea Salad—*
Brings good luck if eaten on New Year's Day

Bowl Game Buffet

Simply Shrimp

Santa Fe Cheesecake

Spicy Glazed Pecans

Black-Eyed Pea Salad

Barbecued Turkey

Pepper-Coated Roast Beef with Red Pepper Basil Butter

Gourmet Potatoes

Haystacks

Turtle Bars

Gram's Best Cookies

Wines: Auslese Riesling, Germany
Gewürztraminer, Alsace
Assortment of domestic and imported beers

Miami Lime Chicken Salad

SERVES 10 TO 12

Creamy Lime Dressing
3/4 cup mayonnaise
Juice of 3 limes (about 6 tablespoons)
1 tablespoon grated lime zest
1 1/2 teaspoons curry powder
1 teaspoon salt
1/4 teaspoon pepper
Salad
2 cups chopped cooked chicken
2 cups cooked rice, chilled
2 green onions, finely chopped
1 cup honeydew melon balls
1 cup cantaloupe balls
2 tablespoons slivered almonds, toasted

For the dressing, combine the mayonnaise, lime juice, lime zest, curry powder, salt and pepper in a bowl and mix well.

For the salad, combine the chicken, rice, green onions, melon balls and almonds in a bowl and mix well. Add the dressing and toss gently to coat. Chill, covered, until serving time. Serve with dillweed bread.

Note: May prepare up to 2 days in advance and store, covered, in the refrigerator.

Chicken Polenta Salad

SERVES 6

Polenta
1 1/4 cups polenta
1 cup shredded Cheddar cheese
1/2 cup sour cream
1 bunch parsley, finely chopped
1 tablespoon kosher salt
1 tablespoon ground black pepper
Salad
3/4 cup olive oil
1/4 cup white wine vinegar
1 to 2 teaspoons Dijon mustard
1/2 teaspoon salt
1/4 teaspoon ground black pepper
1 pound cooked chicken, chopped
3/4 bunch scallions, finely sliced
1/2 cup finely chopped green bell pepper
1/2 cup finely chopped red bell pepper
1/4 cup grated Parmesan cheese
2 ribs celery, finely chopped
1/4 medium red onion, finely chopped
1 tablespoon salt
1 tablespoon ground pepper

For the polenta, bring 4 1/2 cups water to a boil in a large saucepan. Add the polenta gradually, stirring constantly. Boil gently for 5 to 7 minutes, stirring constantly. Stir in the cheese, sour cream, parsley, kosher salt and pepper. Cook for 5 to 7 minutes longer. Spread the polenta on a 9×13-inch baking sheet. Let stand until firm. Cut into 1/2-inch cubes.

Combine the olive oil, wine vinegar and Dijon mustard in a jar with a tight-fitting lid. Cover the jar and shake to blend. Add the salt and pepper. Shake to mix. Combine the chicken, scallions, bell peppers, Parmesan cheese, celery, onion, salt and pepper in a large salad bowl and mix well. Add the polenta and vinaigrette and toss gently to mix.

Empress Chicken Salad

SERVES 6

1 (11-ounce) can mandarin oranges or pineapple chunks
1¹/2 cups mayonnaise
2 teaspoons each curry powder and soy sauce
4 cups chopped cooked chicken or turkey
1¹/2 cups seedless grapes
1 cup chopped celery
1 cup sliced water chestnuts
¹/2 cup slivered almonds, toasted

Drain the mandarin oranges, reserving 2 tablespoons of the syrup. Combine the reserved syrup, mayonnaise, curry powder and soy sauce in a bowl and mix well. Add the mandarin oranges, chicken, grapes, celery, water chestnuts and almonds and toss gently to coat. Chill, covered, in the refrigerator until serving time.

Northern Michigan Chicken Salad

SERVES 8

2 whole boneless skinless chicken breasts, cooked, chopped
³/4 cup cashew halves
³/4 cup dried cherries, coarsely chopped
³/4 cup shredded Cheddar cheese
4 ribs celery, chopped
¹/2 medium red onion, chopped
5 drops of Tabasco sauce
Salt and pepper to taste
Chopped fresh dillweed and basil to taste
Mayonnaise

Combine the chicken, cashews, cherries, cheese, celery, onion, Tabasco sauce, salt, pepper, dillweed and basil in a bowl and mix well. Add just enough mayonnaise to moisten and mix well. Chill, covered, for 4 hours or for up to 2 days before serving.

Shrimp and Avocado Salad

SERVES 6

Ginger Vinaigrette
³/4 cup peanut oil
¹/4 cup fresh lemon juice
3 tablespoons finely chopped canned plum tomatoes
2 tablespoons red wine vinegar
1 tablespoon (rounded) grated gingerroot
1 tablespoon tomato purée
³/4 teaspoon sugar
¹/4 teaspoon salt
¹/4 teaspoon cayenne pepper, or to taste
¹/4 teaspoon ground star anise
Salad
30 large shrimp, peeled, deveined
White wine, beer or water
6 cups watercress or spinach leaves
1¹/2 cups julienned jicama
3 avocados, coarsely chopped

For the vinaigrette, whisk the peanut oil, lemon juice, plum tomatoes, wine vinegar, gingerroot, tomato purée, sugar, salt, cayenne pepper and star anise in a bowl. May prepare 1 day in advance and store in the refrigerator.

For the salad, combine the shrimp with just enough white wine to cover in a saucepan. Poach over low heat for 5 minutes or until the shrimp turn pink; drain. Let stand until cool. Combine the shrimp, watercress, jicama and avocados in a bowl and mix gently. Add the vinaigrette and toss to coat.

Note: Grind the star anise in a small spice grinder or coffee mill. If star anise is not available substitute with Chinese five-spice powder. The shrimp may be poached 1 day in advance and stored, covered, in the refrigerator.

Variation: Add blanched fresh asparagus to the salad, or for a Latin influence, omit the gingerroot and star anise from the vinaigrette and add chopped green chiles.

Elegant . . . but Wild Rice Salad

SERVES 8 TO 10

Salad
2 quarts plus 1 cup water
3 cups wild rice
2 (6-ounce) jars marinated artichoke hearts
1 (10-ounce) package frozen peas
1 green, red or yellow bell pepper, chopped
1 bunch green onions, chopped
1 pint cherry tomatoes, cut into halves

Parmesan Vinaigrette
1^{1}/$_3$ cups vegetable oil
^{1}/$_2$ cup white vinegar
^{1}/$_4$ cup grated Parmesan cheese
1 tablespoon sugar
2 teaspoons salt
1 teaspoon celery salt
^{1}/$_2$ teaspoon ground white pepper
^{1}/$_2$ teaspoon dry mustard
^{1}/$_4$ teaspoon paprika
1 garlic clove, minced

Assembly
^{3}/$_4$ cup slivered almonds, toasted

For the salad, bring the water and wild rice to a boil in a saucepan; reduce heat to low. Simmer, covered, for 45 minutes or until the rice is tender; drain. Drain the artichokes, reserving the marinade for the vinaigrette. Cut the artichokes into halves. Combine the wild rice, artichokes, peas, bell pepper, green onions and cherry tomatoes in a bowl and toss gently.

For the vinaigrette, combine the reserved artichoke marinade, oil, vinegar, cheese, sugar, salt, celery salt, white pepper, dry mustard, paprika and garlic in a jar with a tight-fitting lid. Cover the jar and shake to mix.

To assemble, add half of the vinaigrette to the salad and toss to mix. Add the desired amount of the remaining vinaigrette just before serving. Sprinkle with the almonds. Serve as a salad or side dish along with grilled chicken or fish.

Asian Cabbage Crunch

SERVES 10

Asian Dressing
^{3}/$_4$ cup red wine vinegar
^{1}/$_2$ cup sugar
^{1}/$_2$ cup olive oil
^{1}/$_4$ cup soy sauce

Salad
2 tablespoons butter
2 (3-ounce) packages oriental ramen noodles with seasoning packets, broken
8 ounces sliced almonds
^{1}/$_2$ cup sunflower kernels
^{1}/$_4$ cup sesame seeds
1 small head napa cabbage, shredded or chopped
1 small head red cabbage, shredded or chopped

For the dressing, combine the wine vinegar, sugar, olive oil and soy sauce in a saucepan and mix well. Cook until the sugar dissolves, stirring frequently. Remove from heat. May prepare the dressing 1 day in advance.

For the salad, heat 1 tablespoon of the butter in a skillet until melted. Stir in the noodles and contents of the seasoning packets. Cook until light brown, stirring constantly. Remove the mixture to a bowl.

Add the remaining 1 tablespoon butter to the skillet. Heat until melted. Stir in the almonds, sunflower kernels and sesame seeds. Cook until light brown, stirring constantly. Remove from heat. Combine the cabbage, ramen noodle mixture and almond mixture in a bowl and toss to mix. Add the dressing and mix well.

Black-Eyed Pea Salad

SERVES 8

Vinaigrette
$^2/_3$ cup extra-virgin olive oil
$^1/_3$ cup white wine vinegar
1 garlic clove, crushed
$^1/_2$ teaspoon Dijon mustard
Salt and pepper to taste

Salad
1 large tomato, seeded, chopped
1 green bell pepper, chopped
1 yellow bell pepper, chopped
6 fresh mushrooms, chopped
2 (16-ounce) cans black-eyed peas, drained, rinsed
1 (4-ounce) jar diced pimentos, drained
3 tablespoons chopped fresh cilantro
2 garlic cloves, minced
8 lettuce leaves
8 red cabbage leaves
2 tablespoons crumbled crisp-cooked bacon
$^1/_3$ cup chopped green onions

For the vinaigrette, whisk the olive oil, wine vinegar, garlic, Dijon mustard, salt and pepper in a bowl until mixed.

For the salad, combine the tomato, bell peppers and mushrooms in a bowl and mix gently. Stir in the peas, pimentos, cilantro and garlic. Add the vinaigrette and toss gently to coat. Chill, covered, for approximately 8 hours, stirring occasionally; drain. Spoon the salad onto a serving platter lined with the lettuce leaves and cabbage leaves. Sprinkle with the bacon and green onions.

Tiffany turned to nature for inspiration in all phases of his work. In this necklace, bunches of naturalistically colored nephrite grapes are paired with realistically depicted gold leaves and interlocking links worked to replicate grapevines.

Louis Comfort Tiffany, designer
American, 1848–1933
Tiffany and Company, maker

NECKLACE
Gold with Nephrite Beads, about 1912

Purchased with funds given
by Rita Barbour Kern

57

Corn, Cherry Tomato and Bleu Cheese Salad

SERVES 6

Bleu Cheese Dressing
2 tablespoons balsamic vinegar
$^1/3$ cup olive oil
3 ounces bleu cheese, crumbled
Salad
$2^3/4$ cups cooked fresh corn, or thawed frozen corn
1 pint cherry tomatoes, cut into halves
4 ribs celery, chopped
$^1/2$ large red onion, chopped
2 ($^1/2$-ounce) packages arugula, trimmed, chopped
1 ounce bleu cheese, crumbled

For the dressing, pour the balsamic vinegar into a bowl. Add the olive oil gradually, whisking constantly until blended. Stir in the bleu cheese.

For the salad, combine the corn, cherry tomatoes, celery, onion and arugula in a salad bowl and mix gently. Add the dressing and toss to coat. Sprinkle with the bleu cheese.

Note: May prepare the dressing and salad from 4 to 24 hours in advance and store separately in the refrigerator. Do not assemble the salad more than 4 hours in advance.

Palm Tree Salad

SERVES 6

Lime Mango Dressing
1 teaspoon dry mustard
1 teaspoon sugar
2 tablespoons fresh lime juice
1 tablespoon mango chutney
$^1/2$ cup olive oil
Salt and freshly ground pepper to taste
Salad
1 (14-ounce) can hearts of palm, drained
2 firm ripe avocados, sliced
2 firm ripe mangoes, or 1 cantaloupe, thinly sliced
Juice of $^1/2$ lime
$^1/4$ head iceberg lettuce, finely shredded

For the dressing, combine the dry mustard and sugar in a bowl. Stir in the lime juice and chutney. Add the olive oil gradually, whisking constantly until mixed. Season with salt and pepper. Press the dressing through a strainer to purée the larger pieces of mango and return the mango to the dressing.

For the salad, cut 6 of the large hearts of palm into 1-inch slices. Arrange them on 6 serving plates to represent tree trunks. Cut the smaller hearts of palm into thinner slices to represent coconuts. Arrange alternate slices of the avocados and mangoes at the top of each trunk to represent leaves. Add the coconuts. Drizzle the lime juice over the avocado slices. Arrange some of the shredded lettuce along the bottom of each plate to represent grass. Serve with the dressing.

Riviera Potato Salad

SERVES 6 TO 8

Herb Dressing
1/2 cup olive oil
2 tablespoons each chopped fresh chives and basil
1 tablespoon minced fresh tarragon
1 tablespoon balsamic vinegar
2 teaspoons fresh lemon juice
1 teaspoon Dijon mustard
1 garlic clove, crushed
1/8 teaspoon cayenne pepper

Salad
1 1/2 pounds unpeeled new red potatoes
8 ounces fresh green beans, trimmed, cut into 2-inch slices
1 cup sliced radishes
1 cup cubed feta cheese
3/4 cup sliced black olives
1/3 cup chopped shallots
1/4 cup chopped red bell pepper
1/4 cup chopped fresh parsley
1 (1 1/2-ounce) jar manzanilla green olives, drained, sliced
5 slices crisp-cooked bacon, crumbled
2 tablespoons drained capers
Salt and pepper to taste

For the dressing, combine the ingredients in a blender or food processor container. Process until blended.

For the salad, combine the new potatoes with enough water to cover in a saucepan. Bring to a boil; reduce heat. Cook just until barely tender. Drain and cut into quarters. Blanch the green beans in boiling water in a saucepan for 4 to 6 minutes or until tender-crisp; drain. Plunge into ice water to stop the cooking process; drain.

Combine the new potatoes, green beans, radishes, feta cheese, black olives, shallots, bell pepper, parsley, manzanilla olives, bacon and capers in a bowl and toss gently. Chill, covered, in the refrigerator. Add the dressing and mix gently. Season with salt and pepper.

Pesto Potato Salad

SERVES 8 TO 10

Pesto Sauce
1 cup packed fresh basil leaves
1/2 cup olive oil
2 garlic cloves
1 teaspoon salt
1/2 teaspoon pepper

Salad
2 pounds new red potatoes, cooked, coarsely chopped
1 pound Italian green beans, cooked tender-crisp, drained
1 cup chopped green onions
1/2 cup grated Parmesan cheese

For the sauce, combine the basil leaves, olive oil, garlic, salt and pepper in a food processor container. Process until puréed.

For the salad, combine the new potatoes, green beans, green onions and cheese in a bowl and mix gently. Add the sauce and toss to coat. Spoon into a serving bowl. Garnish with tomato wedges or slices and fresh basil leaves.

Note: May prepare up to 1 day in advance and store, covered, in the refrigerator.

Baby Greens with Warm Hazelnut-Crusted Goat Cheese

SERVES 8

1 (11-ounce) log soft fresh goat cheese, cut into 8 rounds
1 cup finely chopped toasted hazelnuts
1 cup soft fresh French bread crumbs
2 egg yolks
$1/4$ cup water
$1/4$ cup each sherry wine vinegar and olive oil
4 small red onions, thinly sliced
Salt and pepper to taste
$1/4$ cup sherry wine vinegar
2 shallots, minced
$1/2$ cup plus 2 tablespoons olive oil
$1^1/2$ (5-ounce) packages baby greens (15 cups)
3 red apples, thinly sliced
$1/2$ cup hazelnuts, toasted, cut into halves

Pat each goat cheese round $1/2$ inch thick. Combine the finely chopped hazelnuts and bread crumbs in a bowl and mix well. Whisk the egg yolks and water in a bowl until blended. Dip the cheese rounds in the egg mixture and coat with the bread crumb mixture; press lightly. Arrange the rounds in a single layer in a dish. Chill, covered, for 30 minutes or longer.

Preheat the oven to 400 degrees. Whisk $1/4$ cup wine vinegar and $1/4$ cup olive oil in a bowl until blended. Add the onions and toss to coat. Spread the onion mixture on a baking sheet with sides. Sprinkle with salt and pepper. Bake for 30 minutes or until the onions are lightly caramelized, turning frequently.

Whisk $1/4$ cup wine vinegar and shallots in a bowl. Whisk in $1/2$ cup olive oil. Season with salt and pepper. Heat 2 tablespoons olive oil in a heavy skillet over medium-high heat. Add the cheese rounds. Cook for 2 minutes per side or until brown and crisp. Toss the baby greens and apples in a salad bowl. Add just enough of the dressing to coat. Divide the greens and apples evenly among 8 salad plates. Top each salad with 1 cheese round, caramelized onions and hazelnut halves.

Seurat Salad

SERVES 6

1 (14-ounce) can artichoke hearts, drained, sliced
1 (14-ounce) can hearts of palm, drained, sliced
$1/4$ cup chopped green onions
2 tablespoons finely chopped fresh parsley
6 tablespoons salad oil
2 tablespoons fresh lemon juice
Juice of 2 garlic cloves
4 ounces bleu cheese, crumbled
Salt and pepper to taste
Romaine leaves
2 large tomatoes, cut into 12 slices
$1/4$ cup crumbled crisp-cooked bacon

Combine the artichokes, hearts of palm, green onions and parsley in a bowl and mix gently. Add a mixture of the salad oil, lemon juice, garlic juice and bleu cheese and toss to mix. Season with salt and pepper. Chill, covered, in the refrigerator until serving time. The salad may be prepared to this point 1 day in advance.

Line 6 chilled salad plates with romaine. Arrange 2 tomato slices on each salad plate. Top with the artichoke mixture. Sprinkle with the bacon just before serving.

Spinach Salad with Beets and Red Onion

SERVES 6 TO 8

Balsamic Vinaigrette
$3/4$ cup olive oil
$1/4$ cup walnut oil
$1/4$ cup balsamic vinegar
1 medium shallot or scallion, finely minced
$1/8$ teaspoon sugar
Kosher salt and freshly ground pepper to taste

Salad
4 fresh beets, trimmed
6 cups trimmed spinach leaves
1 large red onion, thinly sliced

For the vinaigrette, whisk the olive oil, walnut oil, balsamic vinegar, shallot, sugar, salt and pepper in a bowl.

For the salad, steam the beets until tender; drain. Let stand until cool. Peel and thinly slice the beets. Arrange the spinach on 6 to 8 salad plates. Top with the beets and onion. Drizzle with the vinaigrette. Serve immediately.

Spinach and Feta Salad with Raspberry Vinaigrette

SERVES 6

Raspberry Vinaigrette
$1/4$ cup raspberry vinegar
3 tablespoons extra-virgin olive oil
$1^1/2$ teaspoons honey
$1/8$ teaspoon salt

Salad
$1/2$ cup chopped walnuts
6 cups fresh spinach leaves, torn
2 oranges, peeled, cut into $1/4$-inch slices
4 ounces feta cheese, crumbled
$1/2$ cup raspberries
$1/2$ cup thinly sliced red onion

For the vinaigrette, whisk the raspberry vinegar, olive oil, honey and salt in a bowl.

For the salad, preheat the oven to 350 degrees. Spread the walnuts in a single layer on a baking sheet. Toast for 8 to 10 minutes or until light brown, stirring occasionally.

Toss the walnuts, spinach, orange slices, feta cheese, raspberries and onion in a salad bowl. Add the vinaigrette and mix well. Serve immediately.

B R E A D S &

The recipes featured here are, from top to bottom, Dakota Bread, Morning Glory Muffins, and Tuscan Corn Bread.

Macadamia French Toast

SERVES 4

1 (8-ounce) loaf French bread, cut into 1-inch slices
2/3 cup orange juice
1/3 cup milk
1/4 cup sugar
4 eggs
1 teaspoon grated orange zest
1/2 teaspoon vanilla extract
1/4 teaspoon nutmeg
1/3 cup butter, melted
1/2 cup chopped macadamia nuts

Arrange the bread slices in a single layer in a 9×13-inch baking pan. Whisk the orange juice, milk, sugar, eggs, orange zest, vanilla and nutmeg in a bowl until mixed. Pour over the bread. Chill, covered, for 8 to 10 hours, turning once.

Preheat the oven to 400 degrees. Pour the melted butter onto a 10×15-inch baking sheet with sides, tilting the pan to cover completely. Arrange the soaked bread slices in a single layer on the baking sheet. Sprinkle with the macadamia nuts. Bake for 20 to 25 minutes or until golden brown. Serve with maple syrup and additional melted butter on the side.

Note: Complete the brunch menu with mimosas, Bloody Marys, a bowl of fresh fruit, bacon or sausage and lots of coffee.

Cinnamon Raisin Coffee Cake

SERVES 10

2 cups unsifted flour
1 cup chopped pecans
1/2 cup golden raisins
2 cups sugar
1 cup (2 sticks) butter, softened
2 eggs
1 teaspoon baking powder
1 teaspoon cinnamon
1/2 teaspoon vanilla extract
1/4 teaspoon salt
1 cup sour cream
1/2 cup sugar
1 tablespoon cinnamon

Preheat the oven to 350 degrees. Mix the flour, pecans and raisins in a bowl. Beat 2 cups sugar and butter in a mixing bowl until creamy, scraping the bowl occasionally. Add the eggs, baking powder, cinnamon, vanilla and salt. Beat until blended. Add the flour mixture alternately with the sour cream, stirring well after each addition.

Spoon the batter into a generously greased and floured bundt pan. Bake for 55 to 60 minutes or until the coffee cake tests done. Remove to a serving plate. Sprinkle the warm coffee cake with a mixture of 1/2 cup sugar and cinnamon.

Note: May prepare up to 2 days in advance.

Cranberry Coffee Cake

SERVES 12

Coffee Cake
2 cups flour
1 teaspoon baking soda
1 teaspoon baking powder
1/2 teaspoon salt
1 cup sugar
1/2 cup (1 stick) butter, softened
2 eggs
1 teaspoon almond extract
1 cup sour cream
3/4 cup chopped pecans
1 (16-ounce) can whole cranberry sauce
Confectioners' Sugar Glaze
3/4 cup confectioners' sugar
2 tablespoons warm water
1/4 teaspoon almond extract
1/4 teaspoon vanilla extract

For the coffee cake, preheat the oven to 350 degrees. Mix the flour, baking soda, baking powder and salt together. Beat the sugar and butter in a mixing bowl until creamy, scraping the bowl occasionally. Add the eggs 1 at a time, beating well after each addition. Beat in the flavoring. Add the dry ingredients alternately with the sour cream, beating well after each addition.

Sprinkle the pecans over the bottom of a greased and floured bundt pan. Layer 1/3 of the batter, 1/2 of the cranberry sauce, 1/2 of the remaining batter, remaining cranberry sauce and remaining batter in the prepared pan. Bake for 50 to 55 minutes or until the coffee cake tests done. Cool in pan on a wire rack. Remove to a serving plate.

For the glaze, combine the confectioners' sugar, warm water and flavorings in a bowl, stirring until of a glaze consistency. Drizzle over the coffee cake.

Note: May prepare the coffee cake up to 1 day in advance and store, covered, at room temperature.

Raspberry Danish Coffee Cake

SERVES 12

2 1/4 cups flour
3/4 cup sugar
3/4 cup (1 1/2 sticks) butter, softened
3/4 cup sour cream
1 egg, beaten
1 1/2 teaspoons almond extract
1/2 teaspoon baking powder
1/2 teaspoon salt
1/2 teaspoon baking soda
8 ounces cream cheese, softened
1/2 cup sugar
1 egg, beaten
1/2 cup seedless raspberry jam
1/2 cup sliced almonds

Preheat the oven to 350 degrees. Combine the flour and 3/4 cup sugar in a bowl and mix well. Cut in the butter until crumbly. Reserve 3/4 cup of the crumb mixture. Stir the sour cream, 1 egg, flavoring, baking powder, salt and baking soda into the remaining crumb mixture. Press over the bottom and 3/4 inch up the side of a 9-inch springform pan.

Beat the cream cheese, 1/2 cup sugar and 1 egg in a mixing bowl until blended, scraping the bowl occasionally. Spread in the prepared pan. Top with the jam. Sprinkle with the almonds and reserved crumb mixture. Bake for 45 minutes or until a wooden pick inserted in the center comes out clean and the top is light brown.

Sunrise Coffee Cake

SERVES 12

Coffee Cake
2 cups flour
1 teaspoon salt
1 teaspoon cinnamon
1 teaspoon baking soda
1 teaspoon baking powder
1 cup (2 sticks) butter, softened
1 cup sugar
1 cup packed brown sugar
1 cup buttermilk
2 eggs
2 1/2 cups apple slices or chunks
Streusel Topping
1/2 cup sugar
1/2 cup packed brown sugar
2 tablespoons flour
1 tablespoon butter
1 teaspoon cinnamon
1/2 cup chopped pecans or walnuts

For the coffee cake, preheat the oven to 350 degrees. Sift the flour, salt, cinnamon, baking soda and baking powder into a bowl and mix well. Beat the butter, sugar and brown sugar in a mixing bowl until creamy, scraping the bowl occasionally. Add the buttermilk and eggs and beat until smooth. Add the flour mixture and beat until blended. Stir in the apples. Spoon the batter into a greased 9×13-inch baking pan.

For the topping, combine the sugar, brown sugar, flour, butter and cinnamon in a bowl, stirring until crumbly. Stir in the pecans. Sprinkle over the top of the prepared layer. Bake for 40 minutes.

Royal Scones

SERVES 12

2 cups flour
1/4 cup sugar
1 teaspoon cream of tartar
1/2 teaspoon baking soda
1/4 teaspoon salt
1/2 cup (1 stick) chilled unsalted butter
1/3 cup plain yogurt
1/3 cup dried cherries or currants
1 egg, beaten

Preheat the oven to 325 degrees. Sift the flour, sugar, cream of tartar, baking soda and salt into a bowl and mix well. Cut in the butter until crumbly. Add the yogurt and cherries gradually and stir until mixed.

Knead the dough gently on a lightly floured surface until a ball forms. Shape into 12 equal rounds. Arrange on an ungreased baking sheet. Brush with the egg. Bake for 18 minutes. Serve warm.

Raspberry Butter

MAKES 2 CUPS

2 cups (4 sticks) unsalted butter, softened
1 cup seedless raspberry jam

Combine the butter and jam in a food processor or blender. Process until blended. Store, covered, in the refrigerator. Serve with scones.

Jalapeño Corn Bread

4 slices bacon
2 cups yellow cornmeal
2 teaspoons sugar
1 teaspoon salt
1/2 teaspoon baking soda
1 cup milk
2 eggs, beaten
1 cup chopped onion
1 cup drained whole kernel corn
1/4 cup chopped pimentos
4 jalapeño chiles, minced
1 garlic clove, crushed
8 ounces Cheddar cheese, shredded

Preheat the oven to 350 degrees. Fry the bacon in a skillet until crisp. Drain, reserving 2 tablespoons of the drippings. Crumble the bacon.

Combine the cornmeal, sugar, salt and baking soda in a bowl and mix well. Stir in the milk and eggs until blended. Add the bacon, onion, corn, pimentos, chiles and garlic and beat for 1 minute.

Pour the reserved bacon drippings into a 10-inch cast-iron skillet, tilting the skillet to coat evenly. Layer the cornmeal mixture and cheese 1/2 at a time in the prepared skillet. Bake for 35 minutes. Cut into wedges.

Tuscan Corn Bread

1 cup flour
1 cup yellow cornmeal
2 tablespoons sugar
4 teaspoons baking powder
1/4 teaspoon salt
1 cup milk
1/3 cup grated Parmesan cheese
1/4 cup vegetable oil
2 eggs, beaten
1 cup drained sliced black olives
1 (2-ounce) jar pimentos, drained, sliced
2 tablespoons snipped fresh parsley

Preheat the oven to 425 degrees. Combine the flour, cornmeal, sugar, baking powder and salt in a bowl and mix well. Stir in the milk, cheese, oil and eggs. Fold in the olives, pimentos and parsley.

Spoon the batter into a greased 9×9-inch baking pan. Bake for 20 minutes. Serve immediately.

Unlike Pissarro's familiar, bright Impressionist landscapes, this still life shows the young painter experimenting with bravura brushwork and a limited color range. It has in common with his later works, however, a passionate interest in the everyday world.

Camille Pissarro
French, 1830–1903

STILL LIFE
Oil on canvas, 1867

Purchased with funds from the Libbey Endowment, Gift of Edward Drummond Libbey

Easter Bread

MAKES 3 LOAVES

$1^1/2$ envelopes dry yeast
$1^1/2$ cups warm water
$3/4$ cup sugar
$3/4$ cup vegetable oil
6 eggs, beaten
3 tablespoons plus 1 teaspoon anise oil
$1^1/2$ tablespoons anise seeds
1 tablespoon salt
10 cups flour
1 tablespoon butter, melted

Dissolve the yeast in the warm water in a bowl. Stir in the sugar. Let stand until bubbly. Combine the vegetable oil, eggs, anise oil, anise seeds and salt in a bowl and mix well. Stir in the yeast mixture. Add the flour gradually, stirring constantly until mixed.

Knead the dough on a lightly floured surface until smooth and elastic. Let rise in a warm place for 1 hour. Punch the dough down. Knead lightly. Let rise until doubled in bulk. Punch the dough down.

Divide the dough into 3 equal portions. Shape each portion into a loaf in a greased 5×9-inch loaf pan. Let rise until doubled in bulk. Preheat the oven to 350 degrees. Bake for 25 minutes. Brush the tops of the hot loaves with the butter.

Dakota Bread

MAKES 2 LOAVES

1 envelope dry yeast
1/4 cup honey
1/3 cup warm (100 to 115 degrees) water
2³/4 cups all-purpose flour
1 cup whole wheat flour
1/2 cup cracked wheat
2 teaspoons salt
1 cup cold water
1/4 cup vegetable oil
1 cup unsalted raw sunflower seeds
1/2 cup raw pumpkin seeds
2 tablespoons each sesame seeds, poppy seeds and raw
*   pumpkin seeds*

Stir the yeast and honey into the warm water in a 2-cup measure. Process the all-purpose flour, wheat flour, cracked wheat and salt in a food processor fitted with a metal blade for 5 seconds or until blended. Stir the cold water and oil into the yeast mixture. Pour the yeast mixture through the feed tube in a steady stream, processing constantly until the dough adheres. Process for 45 seconds longer to knead.

Transfer the dough to a lightly floured 1-gallon sealable plastic bag. Squeeze out the air and seal with a wire twist tie. Let rise in a warm place for 1¹/2 hours or until doubled in bulk. Remove the twist tie from the bag and punch the dough down. Combine the sunflower seeds, ¹/2 cup pumpkin seeds, sesame seeds and poppy seeds in a bowl and mix well. Knead the seeds into the dough in the bag. Divide the dough into 2 equal portions. Shape each portion into a round loaf.

Place the loaves on a lightly oiled baking sheet. Let rise, covered with plastic wrap, for 1 hour or until doubled in bulk. Preheat the oven to 375 degrees. Process 2 tablespoons pumpkin seeds in a food processor fitted with a steel blade until coarsely chopped. Sprinkle over the loaves. Bake on the center oven rack for 35 minutes or until light brown. Serve with herb butter.

Cottage Crescents

MAKES 3 DOZEN CRESCENTS

1¹/2 cups cottage cheese
1 cup (2 sticks) butter, softened
2 cups flour
¹/8 teaspoon salt

Beat the cottage cheese in a mixing bowl until smooth. Add the butter, flour and salt. Beat until blended. Chill, covered, for 8 to 10 hours. Let stand at room temperature for 30 minutes.

Preheat the oven to 350 degrees. Divide the dough into 3 equal portions. Roll each portion into a 12-inch circle on a lightly floured surface. Cut each circle into 12 wedges. Roll the wedges up from the wide end. Shape into crescents on a greased baking sheet. Bake for 30 minutes or until golden brown.

Hawaiian Bread

MAKES 1 LOAF

1 cup shredded coconut
2 cups flour
3/4 cup sugar
1 tablespoon baking powder
1/2 teaspoon salt
1 cup milk
1/4 cup vegetable oil
1 egg, beaten
1 teaspoon vanilla extract

Preheat the oven to 350 degrees. Coat the bottom and sides of a 5×9-inch loaf pan with butter and sprinkle lightly with flour. Spread the coconut on a baking sheet. Toast for 3 to 4 minutes or until light brown. Transfer to a bowl to cool.

Add the flour, sugar, baking powder and salt to the coconut. Whisk the milk, oil, egg and vanilla in a bowl until blended. Add to the flour mixture and mix well. Spoon the batter into the prepared pan. Bake for 50 to 60 minutes or until the loaf tests done. Invert onto a wire rack to cool.

Sesame Herb Toast

SERVES 6

1/2 cup (1 stick) butter, softened
2 tablespoons sesame seeds
1/2 teaspoon chopped fresh chervil, or 1/4 teaspoon dried chervil
1/2 teaspoon chopped fresh tarragon, or 1/4 teaspoon
    dried tarragon
1 baguette, cut into 1/2-inch slices

Preheat the oven to 325 degrees. Combine the butter, sesame seeds, chervil and tarragon in a bowl and mix well. Arrange the bread slices in a single layer on a baking sheet. Spread with the butter mixture. Bake until light brown around the edges. Serve with your favorite soups and salads.

Spinach Bread

SERVES 8 TO 10

1 package fresh spinach, trimmed
1 cup milk
3 eggs
1 cup flour
1 teaspoon salt
8 to 12 ounces Monterey Jack cheese, shredded

Preheat the oven to 350 degrees. Rinse the spinach and pat dry. Arrange in a buttered 9×13-inch baking dish. Whisk the milk and eggs in a bowl until blended. Add the flour and salt, whisking until smooth. Pour over the spinach. Sprinkle with the cheese. Bake for 35 to 45 minutes or until brown and bubbly. Serve hot or cold.

Happy Muffins

2 cups flour
$1^1/4$ cups sugar
1 tablespoon cinnamon
2 teaspoons baking soda
2 cups shredded carrots
1 cup shredded zucchini
1 large apple, finely chopped
$3/4$ cup raisins
$3/4$ cup shredded coconut
$1/2$ cup chopped almonds
$1^1/2$ teaspoons grated orange zest
1 teaspoon vanilla extract
1 cup vegetable oil
3 large eggs

Preheat the oven to 375 degrees. Combine the flour, sugar, cinnamon and baking soda in a bowl and mix well. Stir in the carrots, zucchini, apple, raisins, coconut, almonds, orange zest and vanilla.

Whisk the oil and eggs in a bowl until blended. Add to the flour mixture, stirring just until moistened. Spoon $1/4$ cup of the batter into each of 24 greased muffin cups. Bake for 25 minutes.

Morning Glory Muffins

$1^1/4$ cups flour
$1/2$ cup wheat germ
$1/2$ cup packed dark brown sugar
$1/4$ cup oat bran
1 teaspoon baking soda
$3/4$ cup buttermilk
$1/4$ cup canola oil
2 eggs, or $1/2$ cup egg substitute
$1/2$ cup grated carrots
1 (8-ounce) can juice-pack crushed pineapple, drained
1 teaspoon vanilla extract
2 tablespoons sugar
1 tablespoon wheat germ

Preheat the oven to 400 degrees. Line 12 muffin cups with foil liners or spray with nonstick cooking spray. Combine the flour, $1/2$ cup wheat germ, brown sugar, oat bran and baking soda in a bowl and mix well. Whisk the buttermilk, canola oil and eggs in a bowl until blended. Stir in the carrots, pineapple and vanilla. Add to the flour mixture, stirring just until the dry ingredients are moistened.

Spoon the batter into the prepared muffin cups. Sprinkle with a mixture of the sugar and 1 tablespoon wheat germ. Bake for 20 minutes or until a wooden pick inserted in the center of the muffins comes out clean. Remove to a wire rack to cool.

Red, White and Blueberry Muffins

MAKES 1 DOZEN MUFFINS

1/2 cup (1 stick) butter, softened
1 cup sugar
2 eggs
2 teaspoons baking powder
1 teaspoon vanilla extract
1/4 teaspoon salt
2 cups flour
1/2 cup milk
2 cups fresh blueberries
3/4 cup fresh raspberries
1 tablespoon (or more) sugar

Preheat the oven to 375 degrees. Beat the butter in a mixing bowl until creamy. Add 1 cup sugar, beating constantly until pale yellow. Add the eggs 1 at a time, beating well after each addition. Beat in the baking powder, vanilla and salt. Fold in the flour and milk *1/2* at a time. Fold in the blueberries and raspberries.

Spoon the batter into foil-lined muffin cups. Sprinkle with 1 tablespoon sugar. Bake for 25 to 30 minutes or until golden brown. Cool in pan on a wire rack for 30 minutes.

Focaccia alla Griglia

SERVES 6 TO 8

Sun-Dried Tomato Pesto
8 ounces oil-pack sun-dried tomatoes
1/4 cup fresh parsley sprigs
2 shallots, coarsely chopped
1 garlic clove
1 teaspoon balsamic vinegar
Sandwich
1 (1-pound) unpeeled eggplant, cut into 1/3-inch rounds
Coarse salt to taste
Olive oil
*4 red, yellow or orange bell peppers, cut lengthwise
    into halves, seeded*
1 focaccia
Salt and pepper to taste
1 bunch fresh basil
8 slices provolone, mozzarella or fontina cheese

For the pesto, drain the sun-dried tomatoes, reserving 2 tablespoons of the oil. Combine the reserved oil, sun-dried tomatoes, parsley, shallots, garlic and balsamic vinegar in a food processor container. Process until finely chopped. You may prepare in advance and store, covered, in the refrigerator.

For the sandwich, sprinkle both sides of the eggplant with coarse salt. Layer the eggplant in a colander. Let drain for 1 hour. Pat the slices dry with paper towels. Brush each side with a little olive oil. Grill the eggplant and bell peppers over hot coals for 3 to 4 minutes per side or until tender.

Spread the focaccia with the pesto. Arrange the eggplant in slightly overlapping slices over the pesto. Top with the bell peppers. Sprinkle with salt, pepper and basil. Top with the cheese. May be prepared in advance to this point. Bake at 350 degrees until heated through.

Note: Broil the vegetables if time or weather prevents the use of a grill.

Eggs Olé with Red Pepper Cream Sauce—
Featured here as an individual serving

Director's Brunch in the Peristyle Atrium

Melon Ball Cocktail

Tossed Apple Salad

Eggs Olé with Red Pepper Cream Sauce

Elegant Party Casserole

Savory Sausage Ring

Vegetable Gâteau

Cranberry Coffee Cake

Morning Glory Muffins

Wines: Sparkling Wine, California
Sauvignon Blanc, California
Pouilly Fumé, France

Elegant Eggs

SERVES 16

1 (17-ounce) package puff pastry
Flour
1 egg white, beaten
1/4 cup freshly grated Parmesan cheese
4 ounces Swiss cheese, sliced
12 ounces prosciutto, thinly sliced
3 (10-ounce) packages frozen chopped spinach, thawed, drained
1/4 cup minced fresh chives or scallion tops
1 teaspoon salt
1/2 teaspoon each freshly ground pepper and grated nutmeg
1 (8-ounce) can whole pimentos, opened flat, drained, rinsed
2 tablespoons butter
1/4 teaspoon each thyme, basil, oregano and marjoram
12 eggs
1/4 cup heavy cream
1 egg yolk
1/2 teaspoon salt
1 egg, beaten

Roll 1 of the pastry sheets into a 17-inch circle on a lightly floured surface. Roll the remaining sheet into an 11-inch circle. Dust both sides of the pastries with flour. Fit the larger pastry circle into a 10-inch springform pan, allowing a 1/2 inch overhang. Brush the surface of the pastry with the egg white. May prepare in advance to this point and store, covered, in the refrigerator until just before adding the remaining ingredients.

Layer half the Parmesan cheese, half the Swiss cheese and half the prosciutto in the prepared pan. Press the excess moisture from the spinach. Combine the spinach, chives, 1 teaspoon salt, pepper and nutmeg in a bowl and mix well. Spread over the prepared layers. Layer with the pimentos.

Preheat the oven to 425 degrees. Heat the butter in a saucepan until melted. Stir in the thyme, basil, oregano and marjoram. Remove from heat. Whisk 12 eggs, heavy cream, egg yolk and 1/2 teaspoon salt in a bowl until blended. Add to the herb butter and mix well. Cook until of the consistency of scrambled eggs, stirring frequently.

Spread over the pimentos. Layer with the remaining prosciutto, remaining Swiss cheese and remaining Parmesan cheese. Top with the remaining pastry. Fold up the edge of the lower pastry to form a rolled edge. Brush with 1 beaten egg. Make several vents in the top to allow steam to escape.

Bake for 10 minutes. Reduce the oven temperature to 400 degrees. Bake for 35 to 45 minutes longer or until the top is golden brown. Cool in pan on a wire rack for 30 minutes before removing the side of the pan. Cut into wedges with a serrated knife. Serve warm or at room temperature.

Eggs Olé with Red Pepper Cream Sauce

SERVES 8 TO 10

Eggs Olé
1/2 cup flour
1 teaspoon each baking powder and salt
10 eggs
1 pound Monterey Jack cheese, shredded
2 cups creamed, small curd cottage cheese
1/2 cup (1 stick) butter or margarine, melted
2 (2-ounce) cans California green chiles, drained, chopped

Red Pepper Cream Sauce
1 large red bell pepper, chopped
1/4 cup thinly sliced green onions
1/4 cup (1/2 stick) unsalted butter
1/4 cup plus 1 tablespoon flour
1 3/4 cups milk
1 tablespoon fresh lemon juice
1/4 teaspoon each salt and white pepper
2 tablespoons chopped fresh chives

For the eggs, preheat the oven to 350 degrees. Mix the flour, baking powder and salt in a bowl. Beat the eggs in a mixing bowl until light and pale yellow. Add the dry ingredients, Monterey Jack cheese, cottage cheese and butter. Beat until blended. Stir in the chiles. Pour the egg mixture into a 9×13-inch baking dish or eight to ten 4 1/2-inch ramekins. Bake the casserole for 35 minutes or until the top is brown and ramekins until the center appears firm.

For the sauce, sauté the bell pepper and green onions in the butter in a saucepan over medium heat for 2 minutes. Stir in the flour. Cook over low heat for 3 minutes, stirring constantly. Remove from heat. Add the milk and lemon juice gradually, whisking constantly until mixed. Cook until thickened, stirring constantly. Stir in the salt and white pepper. Process in a blender for 2 minutes or until puréed. Puddle the sauce on serving plates. Cut the casserole into squares or invert the ramekins and place over sauce. Sprinkle the chives over the sauce. Garnish with jalapeño and red pepper slices and a sprig of thyme. Serve immediately.

Tapenade-Stuffed Eggs

SERVES 12

Tapenade
1 cup pitted niçoise olives or kalamata olives
4 to 6 tablespoons olive oil
2 tablespoons chopped rinsed capers
2 tablespoons Cognac (optional)
1 tablespoon finely minced garlic
1 tablespoon grated lemon zest or orange zest
1 (2-ounce) can chopped anchovies
1/2 teaspoon freshly ground pepper

Stuffed Eggs
6 eggs
2 tablespoons mayonnaise
Chopped fresh parsley
Shredded romaine (optional)

For the tapenade, combine the olives, olive oil, capers, Cognac, garlic, lemon zest, anchovies and pepper in a food processor container. Process until of the consistency of a coarse paste.

For the eggs, combine the eggs with enough cold water to cover in a saucepan. Bring just to a boil; reduce heat. Simmer over low heat for 8 minutes; drain. Rinse with cold water. Peel the eggs and cut lengthwise into halves. Remove the yolks to a bowl, leaving the whites intact. Add the mayonnaise to the yolks and mash until blended.

To serve, spoon the tapenade and egg yolk mixture side-by-side into each egg white. Sprinkle with parsley. Arrange on a platter lined with shredded romaine.

Note: Leftover tapenade may be spread on toasted bread rounds or used as a topping for roasted tomato halves. May prepare the stuffed eggs up to 1 day in advance and store, covered, in the refrigerator.

Sausage Grits Soufflé

SERVES 10 TO 12

1 pound hot sausage
1 cup quick-cooking grits
6 to 8 eggs, beaten
1 1/2 cups milk
Salt and pepper to taste
2 cups shredded sharp Cheddar cheese
1/4 cup (1/2 stick) butter, melted

Fry the sausage in a skillet, stirring until crumbly; drain. Cook the grits using package directions.

Preheat the oven to 350 degrees. Whisk the eggs, milk, salt and pepper in a bowl until blended. Add to the grits gradually, stirring constantly. Add 1 1/2 cups of the cheese and butter and stir until the cheese melts. Stir in the sausage.

Spoon the grits mixture into a 3-quart baking dish. Bake for 1 to 1 1/2 hours or until set. Sprinkle with the remaining 1/2 cup cheese. Bake just until the cheese melts. Serve immediately.

Note: May prepare 2 to 3 days in advance and store, uncooked, covered, in the refrigerator. Bake as directed.

Vegetable Frittata

SERVES 4 TO 8

1 small yellow onion, coarsely chopped
2 garlic cloves, chopped
1 tablespoon (or more) extra-virgin olive oil
1 cup small broccoli florets
1 cup drained water-pack artichoke hearts, cut into halves
    lengthwise
1/4 cup kalamata olives, pitted, cut into halves
1/4 cup finely chopped red bell pepper
4 sprigs of fresh thyme, minced, or 1 teaspoon dried thyme
4 eggs
1 tablespoon water
1/8 teaspoon salt
3 tablespoons freshly grated Parmesan cheese
Freshly ground pepper to taste
Salt to taste

Cook the onion and garlic in the olive oil in an ovenproof skillet over low heat for 2 to 3 minutes or until the onion is tender, stirring frequently. Stir in the broccoli, artichokes, olives, bell pepper and thyme, adding additional olive oil as needed to coat the vegetables. Increase the heat to high.

Sauté for 3 minutes or until the vegetables are tender and the broccoli is bright green. Remove from heat. Let stand, covered, until needed.

Preheat the oven to 325 degrees. Whisk the eggs, water and 1/8 teaspoon salt in a bowl until blended. Stir in the cheese and pepper. Pour over the vegetables in the skillet. Bake for 15 to 20 minutes or just until the eggs are set. Sprinkle with salt and pepper to taste. Cut into wedges.

Swiss Vegetable Soufflé

SERVES 8 TO 10

3 medium zucchini, cut into $^1/4$-inch slices
1 large sweet onion, cut into $^1/4$-inch slices
3 medium yellow squash, cut into $^1/4$-inch slices
1 red bell pepper, cut into $^1/4$-inch slices
1 yellow bell pepper, cut into $^1/4$-inch slices
8 ounces mushrooms, cut into $^1/4$-inch slices
4 to 5 tablespoons olive oil
6 eggs
$^1/4$ cup heavy cream
8 ounces cream cheese, cubed, softened
2 cups dry bread cubes
2 cups shredded Swiss cheese
2 teaspoons salt
2 teaspoons white pepper
1 teaspoon basil

Reserve several of the zucchini slices for the top. Sauté the remaining zucchini, onion, yellow squash, bell peppers and mushrooms in the olive oil in a skillet over medium heat for 15 minutes or until the vegetables are tender-crisp; drain.

Preheat the oven to 350 degrees. Whisk the eggs and heavy cream in a bowl until blended. Stir in the cream cheese, bread cubes, Swiss cheese, salt, white pepper and basil. Add the vegetable mixture and mix well. Pour into a greased 9-inch springform pan. Arrange the reserved zucchini slices in a decorative pattern over the top. Place the pan on a baking sheet.

Bake for 1 to $1^1/2$ hours or until puffed, brown and firm to the touch, covering with foil during the cooking process if needed to prevent overbrowning. Remove the side of the pan. Cut into wedges. Serve hot or at room temperature.

Note: May prepare 1 day in advance and reheat at 350 degrees for 30 minutes.

Garden Quiches

SERVES 12

4 cups chopped broccoli
4 cups chopped cauliflower
1 cup sliced mushrooms
1 onion, thinly sliced
1 green bell pepper, chopped
1 garlic clove, minced
2 tablespoons vegetable oil
6 eggs, beaten
2 cups (or more) shredded sharp Cheddar cheese
$^1/2$ teaspoon salt
$^1/2$ teaspoon basil, crushed
Curry powder (optional)
2 unbaked (10-inch) deep-dish pie shells

Preheat the oven to 325 degrees. Sauté the broccoli, cauliflower, mushrooms, onion, bell pepper and garlic in the oil in a skillet until tender-crisp. Cover and steam for 2 minutes.

Combine the eggs, cheese, salt, basil and curry powder in a bowl and mix well. Stir into the vegetable mixture. Spoon into the pie shells. Bake for 30 to 40 minutes or until set.

Mushroom Crust Quiche

SERVES 6 TO 8

Mushroom Crust
8 ounces fresh mushrooms, minced
3 tablespoons butter
$1/2$ cup finely crushed saltine crumbs
Filling
$3/4$ cup chopped green onions
2 tablespoons butter
2 cups shredded Monterey Jack cheese or Swiss cheese
1 cup cottage cheese
3 eggs, beaten
$1/4$ teaspoon cayenne pepper
$1/4$ teaspoon paprika

For the crust, preheat the oven to 350 degrees. Sauté the mushrooms in 3 tablespoons butter in a skillet. Stir in the cracker crumbs. Press the mushroom mixture into a greased 9-inch pie plate.

For the filling, sauté the green onions in 2 tablespoons butter in a skillet until tender. Sprinkle over the prepared pie plate. Top with the Monterey Jack cheese.

Combine the cottage cheese, eggs and cayenne pepper in a bowl and mix well. Spoon into the prepared pie plate. Sprinkle with the paprika. Bake for 25 to 30 minutes or until light brown. Let stand for 10 to 15 minutes before serving.

Salmon Mushroom Quiche

SERVES 8

1 recipe (1-crust) pie pastry
4 ounces fresh mushrooms, chopped
2 green onions, minced
2 tablespoons butter
1 (7-ounce) can red sockeye salmon, drained
$1^1/2$ cups heavy cream
3 eggs, lightly beaten
2 tablespoons finely minced fresh chives
1 teaspoon lemon juice
$1/2$ teaspoon salt
$1/8$ teaspoon pepper
$1/8$ teaspoon nutmeg
3 tablespoons shredded Gruyère cheese or Swiss cheese
2 black olives, thinly sliced (optional)
Sprigs of fresh parsley (optional)

Preheat the oven to 400 degrees. Line a 9-inch quiche pan or pie plate with the pastry; trim the edges. Prick the bottom and side of the pastry with a fork. Bake for 3 minutes. Remove from oven. Prick the pastry gently with a fork again. Bake for 5 minutes longer.

Sauté the mushrooms and green onions in the butter in a skillet for 7 minutes. Remove from heat. Combine with the salmon in a bowl and stir until well mixed. Spoon into the baked shell.

Whisk the heavy cream, eggs, chives, lemon juice, salt, pepper and nutmeg in a bowl. Pour over the salmon mixture. Sprinkle with the cheese. Bake for 30 to 35 minutes or until set. Sprinkle with the olives and parsley. Serve immediately as the quiche tends to toughen if reheated.

Spirited Canadian Bacon

SERVES 4

Canadian Bacon

8 (^{1}/2-inch) slices Canadian bacon
^{1}/4 cup packed brown sugar
1 tablespoon dry mustard
8 whole cloves
1 (12-ounce) can ginger ale

Rum Sauce

1 cup water
^{3}/4 cup golden raisins
2 tablespoons dark rum
5 whole cloves
^{3}/4 cup packed brown sugar
2 tablespoons cornstarch
1 teaspoon dry mustard
^{1}/4 teaspoon salt
1 tablespoon butter
1 tablespoon cider vinegar
^{1}/4 teaspoon Worcestershire sauce

For the bacon, preheat the oven to 325 degrees. Arrange the bacon slices in a 9×13-inch baking pan, overlapping if necessary. Combine the brown sugar, dry mustard, cloves and ginger ale in a bowl and mix well. Pour over the bacon. Bake for 45 minutes, basting every 15 minutes.

For the sauce, simmer the water, raisins, rum and cloves in a saucepan for 10 minutes, stirring occasionally. Combine the brown sugar, cornstarch, dry mustard and salt in a bowl and mix well. Sir into the rum mixture. Cook until thickened, stirring constantly; the sauce should be clear and of the consistency of a thick syrup. Stir in the butter, vinegar and Worcestershire sauce.

To serve, drain the bacon. Arrange the bacon on a serving platter. Drizzle with the sauce or serve on the side.

T his elaborate cup, made with the shell of a real ostrich egg, is a prime example of the Renaissance love of rare and exotic items presented in costly and beautifully worked settings. Its main purpose was to impress guests with the owner's wealth and taste.

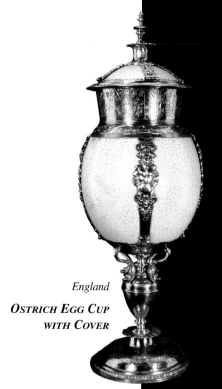

England
**OSTRICH EGG CUP
WITH COVER**

*Silver gilt with
ostrich egg bowl, 1584*

*Purchased with funds from the
Florence Scott Libbey Bequest,
in Memory of her Father,
Maurice A. Scott*

79

Glazed Canadian Bacon

SERVES 4 TO 6

1 pound unsliced Canadian bacon
8 whole cloves
1/4 cup maple syrup
1/4 cup pineapple juice

Preheat the oven to 325 degrees. Arrange the bacon fat side up in a small baking dish. Sprinkle with the cloves. Bring the maple syrup and pineapple juice to a boil in a saucepan. Pour over the bacon. Bake for 1 hour, basting occasionally.

Sweet Mustard Bacon

SERVES 4

8 thick slices bacon
2 teaspoons Dijon mustard
4 teaspoons packed light brown sugar

Preheat the oven to 350 degrees. Line a baking sheet with foil. Place a rack over the foil. Arrange the bacon on the rack. Spread with the Dijon mustard and sprinkle with the brown sugar. Bake for 45 minutes; drain.

Autumn Sausages

SERVES 8 TO 10

2 packages small link sausage
8 Jonathan apples, cored, cut into 1/2-inch rings
3/4 to 1 cup packed brown sugar

Preheat the oven to 350 degrees. Arrange the sausage links in a single layer in a baking dish. Bake for 15 minutes or until brown; drain. Increase the oven temperature to 400 degrees.

Arrange the apples around the sausage. Sprinkle with the brown sugar. Bake for 15 minutes. Reduce the oven temperature to 350 degrees. Bake for 10 to 15 minutes longer or until the sausage is cooked through and the apples are tender, basting with the pan juices frequently.

Savory Sausage Ring

SERVES 12

1 cup fine bread crumbs
1/4 cup chopped fresh parsley
2 eggs, beaten
1 tablespoon grated onion
2 pounds bulk zesty sausage, crumbled

Preheat the oven to 350 degrees. Combine the bread crumbs, parsley, eggs, onion and sausage in a bowl and mix well. Spoon into an 8-cup bundt pan. Bake for 1 hour, draining every 20 minutes during the cooking process. Invert onto a serving platter.

...ff Pancake

...ps milk
1 cup flour
6 eggs
3 tablespoons sugar
1 teaspoon vanilla extract
1/2 teaspoon salt
1/4 teaspoon cinnamon
1/2 cup (1 stick) butter
2 Granny Smith apples, peeled, thinly sliced
3 tablespoons brown sugar

Preheat the oven to 425 degrees. Combine the milk, flour, eggs, sugar, vanilla, salt and cinnamon in a blender container. Process until smooth.

Heat the butter in a 9×13-inch baking dish until melted. Arrange the apples in the prepared baking dish. Bake until the butter sizzles; do not allow the butter to brown. Pour the batter over the apples. Sprinkle with the brown sugar.

Bake on the middle oven rack for 20 minutes or until puffed and brown. Cut into squares. Serve immediately.

Fresh Blueberry Strata

SERVES 6 TO 8

10 slices white bread, crusts trimmed, cubed
4 ounces cream cheese, cubed
1 cup fresh blueberries
1 1/2 cups milk
9 eggs, beaten
1/2 cup half-and-half
1/4 cup maple syrup

Line the bottom of a greased 9×13-inch baking pan with 2/3 of the bread cubes. Sprinkle with the cream cheese and blueberries. Top with the remaining bread cubes.

Whisk the milk, eggs, half-and-half and maple syrup in a bowl until blended. Pour over the prepared layers; press lightly with a spatula. Chill, covered, for 8 to 10 hours.

Preheat the oven to 325 degrees. Bake for 1 hour or until light brown. You may broil briefly to enhance the browning process. Serve with additional warm maple syrup.

VEGETABLES

The recipe featured here
is Country Club Corn Cakes
garnished with caviar, chives
and red bell pepper.

Asparagus Flan

SERVES 6

2 pounds asparagus, trimmed
1/4 cup freshly grated Parmesan cheese
3 tablespoons unsalted butter, softened
2 tablespoons heavy cream
1/2 teaspoon dried tarragon, crushed
1/2 teaspoon salt
3 eggs
1 tablespoon unsalted butter

Butter six 3/4-cup soufflé dishes or custard cups. Line the bottoms of the dishes or cups with rounds of buttered waxed paper. Line a baking pan large enough to accommodate the dishes or cups with a double layer of tea towels.

Cut the tips off the asparagus. Cut the tips lengthwise into halves. Cut the stalks crosswise into 1-inch slices. Steam the asparagus tips, covered, in a steamer rack over boiling water for 1 minute or until tender-crisp. Rinse under cold water in a colander to stop the cooking process. Drain and pat dry with paper towels. Steam the asparagus stalks, covered, in a steamer rack over boiling water for 8 minutes or until tender but bright green. Pat dry with paper towels.

Preheat the oven to 350 degrees. Process the asparagus stalks, cheese, 3 tablespoons butter, heavy cream, tarragon and salt in a blender until puréed. Whisk the eggs in a bowl until blended. Add the asparagus purée gradually, whisking constantly until smooth. Spoon into the prepared soufflé dishes or cups. Arrange in the prepared baking pan. Add just enough hot water to the baking pan to reach halfway up the sides of the dishes or cups.

Bake in the lower third of the oven for 35 to 40 minutes or until a sharp knife inserted in the center comes out clean. Remove the dishes to a wire rack. Let stand for 5 minutes. Heat 1 tablespoon butter in a saucepan until melted. Add the asparagus tips. Cook just until heated through, stirring frequently. Run a sharp knife around the edges of the dishes or cups. Invert the flans onto 6 plates. Top each flan with some of the asparagus tips. Serve immediately.

Oriental Cold Asparagus

SERVES 8 TO 10

Sesame Soy Dressing
1/2 teaspoon sugar
1/4 cup soy sauce
2 teaspoons sesame oil
1/2 teaspoon cider vinegar
Asparagus
2 pounds asparagus, trimmed
Sesame seeds

For the dressing, whisk the sugar, soy sauce, sesame oil and vinegar in a bowl.

For the asparagus, cut the spears diagonally into 1 1/2- to 2-inch pieces. Combine the asparagus with boiling water in a saucepan. Cook for 1 minute or just until barely tender; drain. Rinse with cold water to stop the cooking process; drain.

Toss the asparagus with the dressing in a bowl. Sprinkle with sesame seeds. Chill, covered, for up to 24 hours before serving.

Green Bean Bundles

SERVES 6

1 pound fresh green beans, trimmed
6 slices bacon, partially cooked
3 tablespoons light brown sugar
1 tablespoon prepared mustard
Garlic salt to taste
Pepper to taste

Preheat the oven to 350 degrees. Parboil or steam the green beans until tender-crisp; drain. Gather the beans into 6 bundles, with 7 to 9 beans per bundle. Wrap 1 bacon slice around each bundle. Arrange the bundles in a single layer in a greased baking dish.

Combine the brown sugar, prepared mustard, garlic salt and pepper in a bowl and mix well. Spread over the beans. Bake for 15 to 20 minutes or until the bacon is cooked through.

Note: May prepare up to 1 day in advance and store, covered, in the refrigerator. Bake just before serving.

Honey Nut Green Beans

SERVES 4

1 pound fresh green beans, trimmed
1/3 cup coarsely chopped salted cashews
3 tablespoons unsalted butter
2 tablespoons plus 1 teaspoon honey

Steam the green beans until tender-crisp; drain. Cover to keep warm. Sauté the cashews in the butter in a skillet over low heat for 5 minutes or until light brown, stirring frequently.

Add the honey to the cashew mixture and mix well. Cook for 1 to 2 minutes, stirring constantly. Pour the cashew mixture over the beans in a bowl and toss to coat. Serve immediately.

Carrots Provençale

SERVES 8 TO 10

2 tablespoons extra-virgin olive oil
2 pounds carrots, peeled, diagonally sliced
1 bulb garlic, separated into cloves, cut into halves
Sea salt to taste
30 high-quality black olives, pitted, cut into halves

Heat the olive oil in a skillet over medium-high heat until hot but not smoking. Add the carrots and mix well. Reduce the heat to medium. Braise, covered, for 20 minutes, stirring frequently. Stir in the garlic and sea salt. Reduce the heat to low.

Cook for 15 minutes longer or until the carrots are almost caramelized and the garlic is tender, stirring occasionally. Spoon into a serving bowl. Sprinkle with the olives. Adjust the seasoning. Serve hot or at room temperature.

Black Tie Carrots

SERVES 6

1/2 cup pistachios
2 tablespoons butter
1/4 cup Cointreau
1 pound carrots, cut diagonally into 1/4-inch slices
3 tablespoons butter
3 tablespoons water
1 teaspoon salt

Sauté the pistachios in 2 tablespoons butter in a skillet over medium heat for 1 minute. Stir in the Cointreau. Remove from heat. Combine the carrots, 3 tablespoons butter, water and salt in a saucepan. Bring to a boil over medium-high heat; reduce heat to medium-low.

Cook until the carrots are tender, stirring occasionally. Transfer the carrots with a slotted spoon to a heated serving bowl, reserving the cooking liquid. Cover to keep warm.

Bring the reserved cooking liquid to a boil. Boil until reduced to 2 tablespoons. Drizzle over the carrots. Add the pistachio mixture and toss to coat. Serve immediately.

Country Club Corn Cakes

MAKES 30

4 cups fresh or frozen corn, cooked, drained
1/2 cup heavy cream
1/2 cup flour
4 eggs
1 teaspoon baking powder
1 teaspoon sugar
1 teaspoon salt
1/2 teaspoon white pepper
1/4 teaspoon cayenne pepper
1/4 teaspoon nutmeg
1/4 cup (1/2 stick) unsalted butter or corn oil

Combine the corn, heavy cream, flour, eggs, baking powder, sugar, salt, white pepper, cayenne pepper and nutmeg in a food processor container fitted with a steel blade. Process for 20 seconds or until smooth. Spoon into a bowl. Chill, covered, for several hours to overnight.

Heat the butter in a skillet until melted. Drop the corn batter by tablespoons into the hot butter, forming 2-inch rounds. Cook until the edges turn brown; turn. Cook until light brown; drain.

Note: May freeze the corn cakes for future use. Reheat in a 350-degree oven.

Eggplant Torta

SERVES 4 TO 6

2 large eggplant, peeled
Salt to taste
Olive oil or vegetable oil
1 pound prosciutto, thinly sliced
8 ounces mozzarella cheese, shredded
2 eggs, lightly beaten
$^1/2$ teaspoon dried basil
$^1/2$ teaspoon dried oregano

Cut the eggplant horizontally into $^1/2$-inch slices. Sprinkle both sides of each slice with salt. Arrange in a colander. Drain for 1 hour; pat dry. Add enough oil to a heavy skillet to measure $1^1/2$ inches. Heat to 350 degrees. Fry the eggplant in the hot oil for 2 minutes per side or until golden brown; drain.

Preheat the oven to 375 degrees. Layer the eggplant, prosciutto and cheese alternately in the order listed in a $1^1/2$-quart baking dish, ending with the cheese. Whisk the eggs, basil and oregano in a bowl until mixed. Pour over the prepared layers. Bake for 25 to 30 minutes or until brown.

Serve as a main entrée with a tossed green salad and crusty French bread.

Eggplant Towers

SERVES 6

1 medium eggplant, peeled, cut into $^1/2$-inch slices
1 or 2 large tomatoes, sliced
1 large onion, thinly sliced
$^1/4$ cup ($^1/2$ stick) butter, melted
$^1/2$ teaspoon salt
$^1/2$ teaspoon dried basil
Pepper to taste
4 ounces mozzarella cheese, shredded
$^1/2$ cup dry bread crumbs
$^1/4$ cup ($^1/2$ stick) butter, melted
2 tablespoons grated Parmesan cheese

Preheat the oven to 400 degrees. Arrange the eggplant in a single layer in a baking dish sprayed with nonstick cooking spray. Layer each eggplant slice with 1 tomato slice and 1 onion slice. Drizzle with $^1/4$ cup butter. Sprinkle with the salt, basil and pepper. Bake, covered, for 20 minutes.

Top each layered eggplant slice with some of the mozzarella cheese. Sprinkle with a mixture of the bread crumbs and $^1/4$ cup butter and the Parmesan cheese. Bake for 10 to 15 minutes longer or until light brown. Serve immediately.

C reated for the Portuguese royal court, this display dish shows the current taste for the French Rococo style. Handles imitating intertwining leaves and engravings of vegetables and sea creatures enliven the circumference of the dish, and the Portuguese royal coat of arms occupies the center.

Edmé-Pierre Balzac
French, became Master in
1739; still living in 1781

DISH WITH HANDLES
Silver, 1745–46

Purchased with funds from the
Florence Scott Libbey Bequest,
in Memory of her Father,
Maurice A. Scott

Fennel Gratin

SERVES 6

6 tablespoons unsalted butter
6 large fennel bulbs, trimmed, cored, sliced
$1/2$ cup chicken stock
$1/2$ teaspoon salt
$1/4$ teaspoon freshly ground pepper
Grated nutmeg to taste
$1/2$ cup grated Parmesan cheese
$1/4$ cup toasted bread crumbs
2 tablespoons unsalted butter, melted

Heat 6 tablespoons butter in a large skillet over medium heat until foamy. Add the fennel. Sauté for 10 minutes or until golden brown. Stir in the stock; reduce the heat. Simmer for 15 to 25 minutes or until the fennel is tender, stirring occasionally. Stir in the salt, pepper and nutmeg.

Preheat the oven to 450 degrees. Spoon the fennel mixture into 6 individual gratin dishes or 1 large gratin dish. Sprinkle with the cheese and bread crumbs. Drizzle with 2 tablespoons butter. Bake for 10 minutes or until crusty on top. Serve hot with fish, chicken or beef.

Note: May prepare up to 1 day in advance and store, covered, in the refrigerator. Reheat gently before serving.

Stuffed Portabella Mushrooms

SERVES 6

6 whole portabella mushrooms
1/3 cup Italian salad dressing
1 medium onion, finely chopped
2 tablespoons extra-virgin olive oil
2 garlic cloves, crushed
1/2 cup herb-flavored croutons, crushed
3 tablespoons freshly grated Parmesan cheese
6 fresh basil leaves, chopped
6 tablespoons pine nuts
Grated Parmesan cheese to taste

Remove the stems from the mushrooms and reserve. Chill, covered, in the refrigerator. Combine the mushroom caps and salad dressing in a bowl and toss to coat. Marinate, covered, in the refrigerator for 8 to 10 hours. Preheat the oven to 425 degrees.

Chop the mushroom stems. Sauté the mushroom stems and onion in the olive oil in a skillet. Stir in the garlic. Sauté until the garlic is tender. Remove from heat. Add the croutons, 3 tablespoons Parmesan cheese, basil and pine nuts and mix well.

Drain the mushrooms, discarding the marinade. Arrange stem side up in a greased baking pan. Spoon some of the crouton mixture in each mushroom cap. Sprinkle with Parmesan cheese to taste. Bake for 15 minutes. Serve immediately.

Note: This is good as a side dish with grilled steaks.

Vidalia Onion Pie

SERVES 8

1 tablespoon olive oil
2 pounds Vidalia onions, sliced
1 large shallot, thinly sliced
1/2 cup port
1/2 cup chicken broth or beef broth
1 cup heavy cream
3/4 teaspoon chopped fresh thyme, or 1/2 teaspoon dried thyme
Salt and pepper to taste
1 cup grated asiago cheese
2 large eggs, beaten
1/4 cup chopped fresh parsley
1 unbaked (9-inch) pie shell

Heat the olive oil in a sauté pan over medium heat. Add the onions and shallot and mix well. Cook until tender, stirring frequently. Increase the heat to high. Stir in the port. Cook until reduced by 1/2, stirring frequently. Stir in the broth.

Cook until reduced by 1/2, stirring frequently. Add the heavy cream and mix well. Cook until reduced by 1/2 again, or until the mixture is of the consistency of a cream sauce. Stir in the thyme, salt and pepper. Let stand until cool. Stir in the cheese and eggs. Cool, covered, in the refrigerator.

Preheat the oven to 400 degrees. Spoon the onion mixture into the pie shell. Bake on the bottom oven rack for 1 hour or until set and light golden brown. Garnish with the parsley. Serve warm or at room temperature.

Note: This is a great party dish as it can be prepared in advance.

Gourmet Potatoes

SERVES 6

6 medium red potatoes, peeled
2 cups shredded Cheddar cheese
1/4 cup (1/2 stick) butter
1 1/2 cups sour cream
1/3 cup chopped green onions
1 teaspoon salt
1/4 teaspoon pepper
2 tablespoons butter
Paprika to taste

Combine the potatoes with enough water to cover in a saucepan. Cook until tender but firm; drain. Process in a food processor until grated. Preheat the oven to 350 degrees.

Combine the cheese and 1/4 cup butter in a saucepan. Cook over low heat until the cheese almost melts, stirring constantly. Remove from heat. Stir in the sour cream, green onions, salt and pepper. Fold in the potatoes.

Spoon the potato mixture into a buttered 2-quart baking dish. Dot with 2 tablespoons butter. Bake for 25 minutes or until heated through; do not overcook. Sprinkle with paprika.

Party Potatoes

SERVES 10

8 large potatoes, peeled
3/4 cup sour cream
2 teaspoons salt
1 teaspoon sugar
1/4 teaspoon pepper
Milk
2 (10-ounce) packages frozen chopped spinach
1/2 cup (1 stick) butter, softened
2 tablespoons chopped fresh chives
2 tablespoons chopped green onions
1/2 teaspoon dillweed
1 1/2 cups shredded Cheddar cheese

Combine the potatoes with enough water to cover in a saucepan. Bring to a boil. Boil until tender but firm; drain. Peel the potatoes. Mash the potatoes in a bowl. Stir in the sour cream, salt, sugar and pepper, adding milk as needed for a fluffy consistency.

Preheat the oven to 400 degrees. Cook the spinach using package directions; drain. Press the excess moisture from the spinach. Combine the potatoes, spinach, butter, chives, green onions and dillweed in a bowl and mix well. Spoon into a buttered 9×13-inch baking dish. Sprinkle with the cheese.

Bake for 20 minutes or until brown and bubbly.

Note: May prepare up to 1 day in advance and store, covered, in the refrigerator. Reheat before serving.

Ginger-Sautéed Spinach

SERVES 4

1¹/2 cups fresh orange juice
1¹/2 tablespoons minced gingerroot
1 tablespoon fresh lemon juice
1 pound fresh spinach, trimmed
Freshly ground pepper to taste

Bring the orange juice and gingerroot to a boil in a skillet. Boil until the mixture is reduced to ¹/2 cup. Stir in the lemon juice.

Rinse the spinach; do not drain. Cook the spinach in a large saucepan for 3 minutes or until wilted; drain. Return the spinach to the saucepan. Add the orange juice mixture and toss gently. Sauté for 30 seconds. Season with pepper. Garnish with orange slices.

Note: May prepare up to 1 hour in advance. Reheat before serving.

Spicy Roasted Peppers

SERVES 4

3 roasted red peppers, peeled, cut lengthwise into halves
¹/2 teaspoon salt
¹/2 teaspoon sugar
2 garlic cloves, minced
3 tablespoons olive oil
1 teaspoon balsamic vinegar
Sprigs of fresh rosemary

Preheat the oven to 425 degrees. Arrange the roasted peppers in a single layer in a baking pan. Sprinkle with the salt, sugar and garlic. Drizzle with the olive oil and balsamic vinegar. Top with the rosemary. Bake for 40 minutes.

Butternut Squash Supreme

SERVES 4 TO 6

1 large butternut squash, peeled, cubed (about 6 cups)
Salt to taste
¹/2 cup chopped pecans
3 tablespoons light cream
2 tablespoons butter
1 tablespoon brown sugar
¹/2 teaspoon ground ginger
¹/4 teaspoon salt
¹/4 teaspoon pepper
¹/8 teaspoon nutmeg
¹/4 cup chopped pecans
1 tablespoon butter

Cook the squash in boiling salted water in a saucepan for 20 minutes or until tender; drain and mash. Preheat the oven to 350 degrees.

Combine the squash, ¹/2 cup pecans, light cream, 2 tablespoons butter, brown sugar, ginger, salt, pepper and nutmeg in a bowl and mix well. Spoon into a small baking dish. Sprinkle with ¹/4 cup pecans and dot with 1 tablespoon butter. Bake for 20 minutes.

Tomato and Basil Pie

SERVES 6 TO 8

1 unbaked (9-inch) pie shell
$1/2$ cup shredded mozzarella cheese
5 Roma tomatoes
1 cup loosely packed fresh basil leaves
4 garlic cloves
1 cup shredded mozzarella cheese
$1/2$ cup mayonnaise
$1/4$ cup grated Parmesan cheese
$1/8$ teaspoon white pepper

Preheat the oven to 350 degrees. Prick the side and bottom of the pie shell with a fork. Bake for 15 minutes. Increase the oven temperature to 375 degrees. Sprinkle $1/2$ cup mozzarella cheese over the bottom of the pie shell. Let stand until cool.

Slice the tomatoes. Drain on paper towels. Arrange the tomatoes over the cheese. Process the basil and garlic in a food processor until coarsely ground. Sprinkle over the tomatoes.

Combine 1 cup mozzarella cheese, mayonnaise, Parmesan cheese and white pepper in a bowl and mix well. Spread over the prepared layers. Bake for 35 to 40 minutes or until brown and bubbly. Cut into wedges.

Tally Ho Tomato Pudding

SERVES 6

2 cups bread cubes, crusts trimmed
$1/2$ cup (1 stick) butter, melted
1 cup packed brown sugar
1 cup tomato purée
$1/4$ cup water

Preheat the oven to 350 degrees. Spread the bread cubes in a medium baking dish. Drizzle with the butter.

Combine the brown sugar, tomato purée and water in a saucepan and mix well. Cook for 5 minutes, stirring frequently. Spoon over the bread cubes. Bake for 50 minutes. Serve warm.

Note: This recipe is a Toledo tradition.

Baked Tomatoes

SERVES 8

3 tablespoons cream cheese, softened
3 tablespoons Roquefort cheese
1 teaspoon Worcestershire sauce
$1/2$ teaspoon onion powder
4 medium tomatoes, cut in half crosswise
$1 3/4$ cups soft bread crumbs
Butter
Paprika

Combine the cream cheese, Roquefort cheese, Worcestershire sauce and onion powder in a bowl and stir until blended. Arrange the tomatoes on a baking sheet, cut side up. Spread the cheese mixture over the tomatoes. Sprinkle with the bread crumbs. Dot with the butter. Sprinkle with the paprika. Broil for 10 minutes.

Vegetable Gâteau

Crêpes

2/3 cup milk
2/3 cup water
3 large eggs
1/4 teaspoon salt
1 cup flour
3 tablespoons butter, melted
1 1/2 tablespoons vegetable oil

Custard

1 cup cream cheese, softened
1 cup heavy cream
6 eggs
1/8 teaspoon nutmeg
Salt and pepper to taste

Vegetables and Cheese

1 bunch broccoli, trimmed, separated into florets
6 tablespoons butter, softened
1 pound carrots, peeled, julienned
*1/2 teaspoon dried dillweed, or 1 tablespoon chopped
    fresh dillweed*
Salt and pepper to taste
1 pound mushrooms, finely minced
1/4 cup minced shallots or scallions
2 cups coarsely shredded Swiss cheese

For the crêpes, combine the milk, water, eggs and salt in a food processor container. Add the flour and butter. Process for 1 minute. Chill, covered, for 1 hour or longer. Coat a 6 1/2- or 7-inch cast-iron skillet with the oil. Heat just until the skillet begins to smoke. Pour about 1/4 cup of the batter into the middle of the skillet, tilting the skillet to cover the bottom. Cook for about 1 minute; turn. Cook for 30 seconds longer or until brown. Repeat the process with the remaining batter, stacking the crêpes between sheets of waxed paper.

For the custard, process the cream cheese, heavy cream, eggs, nutmeg, salt and pepper in a food processor until smooth.

For the vegetables and cheese, blanch the broccoli in a small amount of water in a saucepan for 3 minutes; drain. Add 2 tablespoons of the butter and toss to coat. Sauté the carrots in 2 tablespoons of the butter in a skillet. Season with the dillweed, salt and pepper. Sauté the mushrooms and shallots in the remaining 2 tablespoons butter in a skillet. Season with salt and pepper.

To assemble, preheat the oven to 350 degrees. Line a buttered 8-inch springform pan with some of the crêpes, allowing an overhang. Layer with another layer of crêpes. Sprinkle 1/4 of the Swiss cheese over the bottom of the pan. Layer with the carrots. Sprinkle with 1/4 of the remaining Swiss cheese. Add enough of the custard to come up to the level of the carrots. Cover with more of the crêpes. Spread with the mushrooms and shallots. Add enough of the custard to cover the mushrooms. Arrange additional crêpes over the mushroom layer to cover. Sprinkle with 1/2 of the remaining Swiss cheese. Top with the broccoli, remaining Swiss cheese and remaining custard. Fold over the crêpe overhang. Layer with enough crêpes to cover the filling.

Place a sheet of buttered waxed paper over the top. Cover with foil. Bake on the lower middle rack for 1 3/4 hours. Remove from oven. Let stand at room temperature for 10 to 15 minutes. Remove to a platter. Cut into wedges and serve with Plum Sauce (page 18), hollandaise sauce or a light tomato sauce.

Variegated Vegetable Terrine

SERVES 8 TO 12

Spinach Layer
2 (10-ounce) packages frozen spinach, thawed, drained
$1/2$ small onion, minced
3 tablespoons half-and-half
1 egg, beaten
1 teaspoon salt
$1/2$ teaspoon garlic powder
$1/4$ teaspoon white pepper

Cauliflower Layer
1 (10-ounce) package frozen cauliflower, thawed, drained
1 egg, beaten
1 tablespoon half-and-half
1 tablespoon chopped fresh parsley
1 teaspoon salt
$1/2$ teaspoon lemon pepper

Carrot Layer
1 (16-ounce) package frozen carrots, thawed, drained
1 egg, beaten
1 tablespoon half-and-half
1 teaspoon dillweed
$3/4$ teaspoon salt
$1/2$ teaspoon ground ginger

For the spinach layer, press the spinach to remove the excess moisture. Combine the spinach, onion, half-and-half, egg, salt, garlic powder and white pepper in a food processor container. Process until smooth. Spoon into a greased 5×9-inch loaf pan.

For the cauliflower layer, press the cauliflower to remove the excess moisture. Combine the cauliflower, egg, half-and-half, parsley, salt and lemon pepper in a food processor container. Process until smooth. Spread over the spinach layer.

For the carrot layer, process the carrots, egg, half-and-half, dillweed, salt and ginger in a food processor until puréed. Spread over the cauliflower layer. Cover with buttered waxed paper.

Preheat the oven to 325 degrees. Place the loaf pan in a larger baking pan. Add enough water to the larger baking pan to measure 1 to 2 inches. Bake for 1 to $1^1/2$ hours or until set. Cool slightly. Invert onto a serving platter. Garnish with carrot flowers. Serve warm.

Yams with Candied Apples and Cranberries

SERVES 6 TO 8

3 large yams or sweet potatoes, peeled, chopped
1 medium Golden Delicious apple, peeled, chopped
1 cup fresh or frozen cranberries
$3/4$ cup packed brown sugar
1 teaspoon cinnamon
$1/4$ teaspoon nutmeg
$1/3$ cup orange juice or orange liqueur
$1/2$ cup chopped pecans, toasted

Combine the yams and apple in a slow cooker. Add the cranberries. Sprinkle with a mixture of the brown sugar, cinnamon and nutmeg. Drizzle with the orange juice. Cook on Low for $8^1/2$ to 10 hours, stirring occasionally. Spoon into a serving bowl. Sprinkle with the pecans. Double the recipe for a large crowd and cook in a 5-quart slow cooker.

P

olka-Dot Noodles—
Simple and yummy

Dinner on the Terrace

Sicilian Salsa

Feta with Pepper Honey

Bloody Mary Aspic

Salmon with Pineapple Salsa

Green Bean Bundles

Polka-Dot Noodles

Key Lime Cheesecake

Wines: Pinot Grigio, Italy
Pinot Noir, California

Asparagus Farfalle Pasta

SERVES 4 TO 6

1 tablespoon light olive oil
2 medium garlic cloves, minced
3 boneless skinless chicken breast halves, chopped
1 tablespoon olive oil
1 teaspoon (heaping) brown sugar
12 to 15 asparagus spears, diagonally sliced into 2-inch pieces
16 ounces farfalle
1/4 cup (1/2 stick) butter
1/4 cup olive oil
3/4 cup freshly grated asiago cheese
3 tablespoons drained capers
Salt and pepper to taste
1 cup fresh basil leaves
3/4 cup freshly grated asiago cheese

Heat 1 tablespoon light olive oil in a skillet over medium-high heat until hot. Add the garlic. Sauté until light brown. Add the chicken. Cook until the chicken is tender, stirring frequently. Remove the chicken to a serving platter using a slotted spoon. Cover to keep warm.

Heat 1 tablespoon olive oil in a skillet over medium-high heat until hot. Spoon the brown sugar in a circle in the center of the prepared skillet. Cook until the edge of the brown sugar just starts to bubble; do not stir. Add the asparagus. Cook for 1 minute, stirring constantly. Remove from heat. Let stand in the skillet, covered, for 25 minutes.

Cook the pasta using package directions. Drain and rinse. Return the pasta to the saucepan. Add the butter and 1/4 cup olive oil and toss to coat. Stir in 3/4 cup cheese and capers gently. Add the asparagus, chicken, salt and pepper and mix well. Spoon into a serving bowl. Sprinkle with the basil and 3/4 cup cheese.

Black Bean Pasta

SERVES 4

4 large tomatoes
1 (16-ounce) can black beans, drained, rinsed
1/4 cup extra-virgin olive oil
4 garlic cloves, minced
3 tablespoons chopped fresh cilantro
2 tablespoons chopped fresh chives
2 tablespoons fresh lime juice
3/4 teaspoon chili powder
1/2 teaspoon salt
1/4 teaspoon pepper
8 ounces thin spaghetti, cooked, drained
1 cup shredded Monterey Jack cheese

Peel the tomatoes and chop, reserving the juice. Combine the tomatoes, reserved juice, beans, olive oil, garlic, cilantro, chives, lime juice, chili powder, salt and pepper in a bowl and mix well. Let stand, covered, at room temperature for up to 5 hours, stirring occasionally. Spoon over hot cooked spaghetti on a serving platter. Sprinkle with the cheese.

Cobb Rotini

SERVES 6 TO 8

Honey Dijon Vinaigrette
1 cup olive oil
1/4 cup balsamic vinegar
1 teaspoon Dijon mustard
1 teaspoon honey
1 garlic clove, minced
1/2 teaspoon pepper

Pasta
8 ounces shell or wagon wheel pasta, cooked al dente, drained
2 cups chopped cooked chicken
12 ounces bacon, crisp-cooked, crumbled
2 tomatoes, chopped
2 cups fresh baby spinach
1 cup black olives, cut into halves
4 ounces Gorgonzola cheese, crumbled

For the vinaigrette, whisk the olive oil, balsamic vinegar, Dijon mustard, honey, garlic and pepper in a bowl until mixed.

For the pasta, combine the pasta, chicken, bacon, tomatoes, spinach, black olives and cheese in a large bowl and mix well. Add the vinaigrette and toss to coat. Chill, covered, until serving time.

Fruit and Noodles in Pecan Crust

SERVES 8

8 ounces medium noodles, cooked, drained
2 tablespoons butter, melted
1 apple, peeled, sliced
8 dried apricots, coarsely chopped
1/4 cup raisins
1/4 cup sugar
2 eggs, lightly beaten
1/4 teaspoon cinnamon
1/4 cup (1/2 stick) butter, melted
1/2 cup packed brown sugar
1 cup coarsely chopped pecans

Toss the noodles with 2 tablespoons butter in a bowl. Combine the apple, apricots, raisins, sugar, eggs and cinnamon in a bowl and mix well. Fold into the noodles. Chill, covered, for 2 hours. Preheat the oven to 350 degrees. Brush the bottom and side of a round 2-quart baking dish with 1/4 cup melted butter. Sprinkle with the brown sugar and pecans. Spoon the noodle mixture into the prepared dish. Bake for 1 1/2 hours.

Polka-Dot Noodles

SERVES 8 TO 10

16 ounces noodles
1 cup (2 sticks) butter
1 1/2 cups blanched slivered almonds
1/2 cup poppy seeds
3/4 teaspoon salt

Cook the noodles using package directions; drain. Cover to keep warm. Heat the butter in a skillet over low heat until melted. Stir in the almonds. Cook until golden brown, stirring frequently. Stir in the poppy seeds and salt. Add to the noodles and toss gently to mix.

Noodle Pudding with Crunchy Topping

SERVES 16

8 ounces broad noodles
1 cup (2 sticks) butter, softened
16 ounces cream cheese, softened
2 cups sour cream
1 1/2 cups sugar
8 eggs
2 tablespoons lemon juice
1 teaspoon grated lemon zest
1 cup graham cracker crumbs
1/4 cup sugar
1 teaspoon cinnamon
1/4 cup (1/2 stick) butter, melted
1/2 cup fresh orange juice, at room temperature

Cook the noodles using package directions; drain. Add 1 cup butter and mix until coated. Spoon the noodle mixture into a buttered 9×13-inch baking dish. Chill, covered, for 1 hour or longer. Beat the cream cheese, sour cream, 1 1/2 cups sugar, eggs, lemon juice and lemon zest in a mixing bowl until smooth, scraping the bowl occasionally. Spoon over the noodles.

Preheat the oven to 350 degrees. Combine the graham cracker crumbs, 1/4 cup sugar and cinnamon in a bowl and mix well. Add melted butter and stir until crumbly. Sprinkle over the top of the noodle mixture. Bake for 25 to 30 minutes. Pour the orange juice over the top. Bake for 25 to 30 minutes longer or until set.

Thai Pasta

SERVES 6

Peanut Dressing
1/2 cup peanut butter
6 tablespoons red wine vinegar
1/4 cup soy sauce
2 tablespoons vegetable oil
4 teaspoons grated gingerroot
2 large garlic cloves, crushed
1 1/2 to 2 teaspoons Szechuan chili paste
1 teaspoon sugar
1 teaspoon sesame oil
1/2 cup water
Salt to taste
Pasta
1 head iceberg lettuce
4 ounces fresh angel hair pasta
1 pound boneless skinless chicken breasts, cooked, shredded
1/2 cup julienned carrots, cooked, drained
1/2 cup julienned green onions with tops
1/2 cup julienned cucumber
1/2 cup julienned red bell pepper
1/2 cup fresh bean sprouts
1/2 cup shredded coconut, or to taste

For the dressing, whisk the peanut butter, wine vinegar, soy sauce, vegetable oil, gingerroot, garlic, chili paste, sugar and sesame oil in a bowl. Stir in the water. Season with salt. May prepare 1 day in advance and store, covered, in the refrigerator.

For the pasta, reserve several whole lettuce leaves. Shred the remaining lettuce. Cook the pasta using package directions; drain. Rinse with cold water; drain. Chill the pasta, chicken, carrots, green onions, cucumber, bell pepper and bean sprouts in separate containers in the refrigerator.

Arrange the whole lettuce leaves on a serving platter. Layer with the shredded lettuce, pasta, chicken, carrot, green onions, cucumber, bell pepper and bean sprouts in the order listed. Drizzle with the dressing. Sprinkle with the coconut.

Salmon and Pasta Rags

SERVES 6 TO 8

1/4 cup white wine
1 tablespoon honey
1 teaspoon Dijon mustard
1 garlic clove, crushed
1 pound salmon fillets
1 red bell pepper, chopped
1 small onion, chopped
6 quarts water
2 tablespoons plus 1 teaspoon salt
8 ounces lasagna noodles, broken into irregular pieces
8 ounces trinette noodles, broken into irregular pieces
6 tablespoons extra-virgin olive oil
1 cup chopped seeded tomato
1/2 cup chopped sun-dried tomatoes
1/4 cup chopped fresh dillweed
1/2 teaspoon pepper

Combine the white wine, honey, Dijon mustard and garlic in a bowl and mix well. Pour over the salmon in a sealable plastic bag. Marinate in the refrigerator for 3 hours. Sauté the bell pepper and onion in a nonstick skillet until tender.

Bring the water and 2 tablespoons of the salt to a boil in a saucepan. Add the pasta. Cook using package directions. Drain, reserving 1 cup of the cooking liquid; do not rinse the pasta. Toss the pasta with the olive oil in a bowl. Stir in the bell pepper mixture, remaining 1 teaspoon salt, tomato, sun-dried tomatoes, dillweed and pepper. Add some of the reserved liquid if needed for moistness and mix gently. Cover to keep warm.

Preheat the oven to 350 degrees. Drain the fillets. Arrange in a single layer on a baking sheet. Bake for 20 minutes or until the fish flakes easily with a fork. Flake the salmon and add to the pasta mixture. Toss to mix. Serve immediately.

Note: Bake the salmon when boiling the pasta, so the pasta dish can be mixed immediately.

Mandarin Shrimp Pasta

SERVES 4

1 pound medium shrimp, peeled, deveined
6 green onions with tops, chopped
1 cup Italian salad dressing
2 tablespoons peanut butter
1 tablespoon soy sauce
1 tablespoon honey
1 (1-inch) piece gingerroot, grated
1/2 teaspoon crushed red pepper
1 tablespoon vegetable oil
1 tablespoon sesame oil
1 medium carrot, peeled, shredded
12 ounces angel hair pasta, cooked, drained
3 tablespoons chopped fresh cilantro
1 (11-ounce) can mandarin oranges, drained
1/3 cup almonds, toasted

Combine the shrimp and green onions with 1/3 cup of the salad dressing in a bowl and toss to mix. Marinate, covered, in the refrigerator for 1 hour. Combine the remaining 2/3 cup salad dressing, peanut butter, soy sauce, honey, gingerroot and red pepper in a bowl and mix well.

Heat the vegetable oil and sesame oil in a skillet until hot. Add the carrot. Cook for 1 minute, stirring frequently. Drain the shrimp mixture, discarding the marinade. Add to the carrot mixture and mix well. Cook for 3 minutes or until the shrimp turn pink, stirring frequently. Remove from heat.

Combine the shrimp mixture, peanut butter mixture, pasta and cilantro in a bowl and toss gently. Top with the oranges. Sprinkle with the almonds. Serve hot or chilled.

Orzotto with Wild Mushrooms

SERVES 8

1/3 cup finely chopped shallots
3 tablespoons olive oil
12 ounces orzo
2 tablespoons Cognac
3 1/2 to 4 cups beef broth
4 ounces shiitake mushrooms, sliced
1/2 cup heavy cream
1/4 cup grated Parmesan cheese
Sprigs of parsley

Sauté the shallots in the olive oil in a large saucepan until tender. Stir in the orzo. Sauté for 5 minutes or until light brown. Reduce the heat. Stir in the Cognac. Cook until the liquid is absorbed, stirring constantly. Add 1 cup of the broth and mix well.

Cook over low heat until the broth is absorbed, stirring constantly. Add another cup of the broth. Cook until the broth is absorbed, stirring constantly. Stir in the mushrooms and remaining broth. Cook until the broth is absorbed and the orzo is tender. Add the heavy cream and mix well. Stir in the cheese just before serving. Spoon into a serving bowl. Top with the parsley.

Orzo and Wild Rice Pilaf

SERVES 6

1 large onion, chopped
1 rib celery, finely chopped
2 teaspoons vegetable oil
1 1/4 cups wild rice, rinsed, drained
2 3/4 cups chicken stock, boiling
1 sprig of fresh thyme, or 1/2 teaspoon dried thyme
1/2 cup orzo
Salt to taste
2 tablespoons finely chopped scallions
2 tablespoons finely chopped fresh Italian parsley
1 teaspoon grated orange zest
Freshly ground pepper to taste
1/4 cup chopped pecans or almonds, toasted (optional)

Sauté the onion and celery in the oil in a saucepan over medium heat for 5 minutes or until tender. Stir in the wild rice, stock and thyme. Bring to a simmer, stirring occasionally. Reduce the heat to medium-low. Cook, covered, for 50 minutes or until the rice is tender and all the liquid is absorbed.

Cook the orzo in lightly salted boiling water in a saucepan for 7 minutes or just until tender; do not overcook. Drain in a sieve and rinse with warm water. Stir the orzo, scallions, parsley and orange zest into the wild rice mixture. Season with salt and pepper. Spoon into a serving bowl. Sprinkle with the pecans.

*Note:*May prepare up to 2 days in advance and store, covered, in the refrigerator. Reheat, covered, in a baking dish sprayed with nonstick cooking spray at 325 degrees for 20 minutes or until heated through. Add a small amount of orange juice if needed to moisten.

Orzo Athena

SERVES 8

12 ounces orzo
2 tablespoons olive oil
1 tablespoon lemon juice
3 tablespoons white wine vinegar
1 teaspoon Dijon mustard
1 small garlic clove, minced
$^1/_2$ teaspoon oregano
$^1/_4$ teaspoon cumin
$^1/_8$ teaspoon thyme
Salt and freshly ground pepper to taste
$^1/_2$ cup olive oil
2 bunches fresh spinach, trimmed, torn into bite-size pieces
$^1/_2$ cup pitted kalamata olives, slivered
1 red bell pepper, julienned
2 to 4 green onions with tops, minced
1 tablespoon rinsed drained capers
2 to 4 ounces feta cheese, crumbled

Cook the orzo using package directions; drain. Rinse with cold water and drain. Combine the orzo with 2 tablespoons olive oil in a bowl and mix well. Combine the lemon juice, wine vinegar, Dijon mustard, garlic, oregano, cumin, thyme, salt, pepper and $^1/_2$ cup olive oil in a bowl and mix well.

Stir the mustard mixture into the orzo mixture. Add the spinach, olives, bell pepper, green onions and capers and mix well. Add the cheese and toss to mix. Spoon onto 8 salad plates.

Note: Add cooked shrimp or cooked chicken for a more hearty salad. May prepare the salad 3 to 4 hours in advance and store, covered, in the refrigerator, adding the cheese just before serving.

This pitcher comes from a long tradition of vessels imitating the forms of the natural world. In a humorous variation on the traditional hobnailed surface of milk glass, the artist has imitated corn kernels and added realistic leaves growing up from the base.

*New England Glass Works,
W. L. Libbey and Son
Glass Company
Toledo, Ohio*

PITCHER
Maize glass, 1889–1890

*Purchased with funds from the
Libbey Endowment, Gift of
Edward Drummond Libbey*

Couscous with Orange and Garlic

SERVES 6 TO 8

$1^1/2$ cups couscous
$1/2$ cup raisins
1 teaspoon turmeric
2 cups boiling water
1 (15-ounce) can chick-peas, drained, rinsed
2 medium tomatoes, seeded, chopped
$2/3$ cup sliced almonds, toasted
3 scallions, thinly sliced
$1/3$ cup lemon juice
$1/3$ cup olive oil
2 garlic cloves, minced
Grated zest of 1 orange
1 tablespoon minced fresh basil
$1/2$ teaspoon salt
Freshly ground pepper to taste
Green leaf lettuce

Combine the couscous, raisins and turmeric in a heatproof bowl. Add the boiling water, stirring until mixed. Let stand, covered, for 5 minutes. Fluff with a fork. Let stand, covered, for 10 minutes longer. Stir in the chick-peas, tomatoes, almonds and scallions.

Whisk the lemon juice, olive oil, garlic, orange zest, basil, salt and pepper in a bowl. Add to the couscous mixture and toss to coat. Chill, covered, for 30 minutes or for up to 24 hours. Spoon onto lettuce-lined salad plates.

Note: May double or triple the recipe for larger crowds. Great for vegetarians.

Moroccan Vegetable Couscous

SERVES 8

2 cups quick-cooking couscous
$1/2$ cup dried currants
$1^1/3$ cups boiling chicken stock
2 medium zucchini
6 medium green onions
2 large shallots
$1/4$ cup extra-virgin olive oil
$1/4$ cup safflower oil
$1/3$ cup pine nuts
1 teaspoon salt
2 small red bell peppers, cut into 1-inch pieces
4 to 5 tablespoons fresh lemon juice
1 teaspoon cumin

Combine the couscous and currants in a heatproof bowl and mix well. Add the boiling stock and stir until mixed. Let stand for 5 minutes.

Cut the zucchini lengthwise into halves; remove the seeds. Remove the pulp and cut into 1-inch pieces. Process the green onions and shallots in a food processor until minced. Add the zucchini. Pulse twice or until coarsely chopped.

Heat the olive oil and safflower oil in a 10-inch skillet over medium heat. Add the pine nuts. Cook for 5 minutes or until golden brown, stirring frequently. Remove the pine nuts with a slotted spoon to a bowl, reserving the pan drippings. Stir the zucchini mixture and salt into the reserved pan drippings. Increase the heat to high. Cook for 2 minutes or until the vegetables begin to soften, stirring frequently.

Process the bell peppers in a food processor until finely chopped. Stir into the zucchini mixture. Cook for 1 minute, stirring frequently. Add the couscous mixture, lemon juice and cumin and mix well. Cook for 1 minute or until heated through, stirring frequently. Remove from heat. Stir in the pine nuts. Adjust the seasonings. Serve hot, cold or at room temperature. May prepare up to 3 days in advance and store, covered, in the refrigerator.

Peruvian Quinoa

SERVES 4

2 tablespoons unsalted butter
2 shallots, chopped
2 small carrots, peeled, chopped
1²/3 cups rich chicken stock
²/3 cup quinoa
1/4 teaspoon cumin
Salt and freshly ground pepper to taste
Chopped fresh parsley

Heat the butter in a medium saucepan over medium-low heat until melted. Stir in the shallots. Cook for 1 minute, stirring constantly. Add the carrots and mix well. Cook for 1 minute longer, stirring constantly. Increase the heat to high. Stir in ²/3 cup of the stock. Bring to a boil; reduce heat.

Cook, covered, over medium-low heat for 15 minutes. Spoon the mixture into a food processor container. Process until smooth. Transfer the mixture to a clean saucepan.

Rinse the quinoa with cold water; drain. Add the remaining 1 cup stock to the carrot mixture. Bring to a boil over high heat. Stir in the quinoa. Reduce the heat to medium-low.

Simmer, covered, for 12 to 15 minutes or until the quinoa is tender. Stir in the cumin, salt and pepper. Spoon into a serving bowl. Sprinkle with parsley.

Note: Quinoa has been called the "mother grain of the Incas." A gluten-free, complete protein, quinoa is grown in the Andes of Bolivia and Peru. Its popularity is increasing, especially in the chic new restaurants in New York, Chicago and Los Angeles, where it is served with Thai peppers, lime juice and coriander, or lemon grass and snow peas.

Citrus Wild Rice

SERVES 4 OR 5

1 cup wild rice
2 large oranges
1/3 cup raisins
1/2 cup fresh orange juice
2 tablespoons capers
1¹/2 tablespoons extra-virgin olive oil
1¹/2 tablespoons balsamic vinegar
Salt and freshly ground pepper to taste
3 scallions, finely chopped
1/2 bunch Italian parsley, finely chopped
Sprigs of assorted fresh herbs

Cook the wild rice using package directions. Peel the oranges and remove the white pithy membrane. Cut between the membranes to remove the sections, reserving several whole sections for garnish. Chop the remaining sections.

Soak the raisins in the orange juice in a bowl for 5 minutes. Whisk in the capers, olive oil, balsamic vinegar, salt and pepper. Stir in the scallions, parsley, rice and chopped orange sections. Mound the rice on a serving platter. Top with the reserved orange sections and sprigs of fresh herbs. Serve with teriyaki chicken or pork or with duck.

Island Rice

SERVES 6 TO 8

2 cups chopped celery
1 small onion, chopped
2 garlic cloves, minced
1 tablespoon butter
4 cups water
$1/2$ cup raisins
2 chicken bouillon cubes
1 tablespoon brown sugar
1 teaspoon curry powder
$1/4$ teaspoon salt
$1/4$ teaspoon cinnamon
$1/4$ teaspoon pepper
$1^1/2$ cups basmati rice
$1/2$ cup chopped pecans
$1/2$ cup chopped apple

Sauté the celery, onion and garlic in the butter in a skillet until the vegetables are tender. Add the water, raisins, bouillon cubes, brown sugar, curry powder, salt, cinnamon and pepper and mix well. Bring to a boil, stirring occasionally. Stir in the rice; reduce heat.

Simmer, covered, for 20 minutes or until the liquid is absorbed. Remove from heat. Let stand for 10 minutes. Stir in the pecans and apple. Garnish with additional pecans and additional raisins.

Greek Rice

SERVES 6 TO 8

4 ounces mushrooms, sliced
1 medium onion, chopped
1 garlic clove, minced
$1/4$ cup ($1/2$ stick) butter
1 (10-ounce) package frozen chopped spinach, thawed
3 cups cooked rice
4 ounces feta cheese, crumbled
3 tablespoons lemon juice
$1/2$ teaspoon dillweed

Preheat the oven to 350 degrees. Sauté the mushrooms, onion and garlic in the butter in a large skillet until the vegetables are tender. Press the excess moisture from the spinach. Add the spinach, rice, cheese, lemon juice and dillweed to the mushroom mixture and mix well.

Spoon the rice mixture into a buttered 2-quart baking dish. Bake for 25 minutes or until heated through.

Yellow Pepper Risotto

SERVES 4

3 yellow bell peppers, chopped
2 tablespoons unsalted butter
1 tablespoon water
Salt and pepper to taste
1 cup finely chopped zucchini
1 tablespoon unsalted butter
6 shallots, minced
1 garlic clove
2 tablespoons unsalted butter
1 cup arborio rice
1/3 cup dry white wine
4 cups simmering chicken broth
1 cup freshly grated Parmesan cheese
2 tablespoons minced Italian parsley

Combine the bell peppers, 2 tablespoons butter and water in a skillet. Cook, loosely covered, over medium heat for 20 minutes or until tender, stirring occasionally. Process the bell pepper mixture in a food processor or blender until puréed. Strain through a coarse sieve into a bowl. Season with salt and pepper. Cook the zucchini in 1 tablespoon butter in a skillet over medium heat for 2 minutes or until tender-crisp, stirring constantly. Season with salt and pepper.

Cook the shallots and garlic in 2 tablespoons butter in a saucepan over medium-low heat for 5 minutes or until tender but not brown, stirring frequently. Stir in the rice. Cook over medium heat for 5 minutes or until the edges of the rice become translucent, stirring constantly. Stir in the wine. Cook until the wine is absorbed, stirring constantly. Add 1/2 cup of the broth and mix well. Cook until the broth is absorbed, stirring

constantly. Add the remaining broth 1/2 cup at a time, cooking until the broth is absorbed after each addition and stirring constantly. Remove from heat. Stir in the bell pepper purée, zucchini, cheese and 1 tablespoon of the parsley. Season with salt and pepper. Spoon into a serving bowl. Sprinkle with the remaining 1 tablespoon parsley. Serve immediately.

Lemon and Herb Risotto Cake

SERVES 4 TO 6

1 small leek, thinly sliced
2 1/2 cups chicken broth
1 cup arborio rice or other short grain rice
Finely grated zest of 1 lemon
2 tablespoons chopped fresh chives
2 tablespoons chopped fresh parsley
1/4 cup shredded mozzarella cheese
Salt and pepper to taste

Combine the leek and 3 tablespoons of the broth in a saucepan. Cook over medium heat until tender, stirring frequently. Stir in the remaining broth and rice. Bring to a boil; reduce heat. Simmer, covered, for 20 minutes or until the liquid is absorbed, stirring occasionally. Preheat the oven to 400 degrees.

Stir the lemon zest, chives, parsley, cheese, salt and pepper into the rice mixture. Spoon into an oiled 8 1/2-inch springform pan. Bake, covered with foil, for 30 to 35 minutes or until light brown, removing the foil 15 minutes before the end of the cooking process. Remove the side of the pan. Cut into wedges. Garnish with sprigs of parsley and lemon slices. Serve hot or chilled. Serve larger portions with a salad as an entrée.

The recipe featured here is
Salmon with Pineapple Salsa.

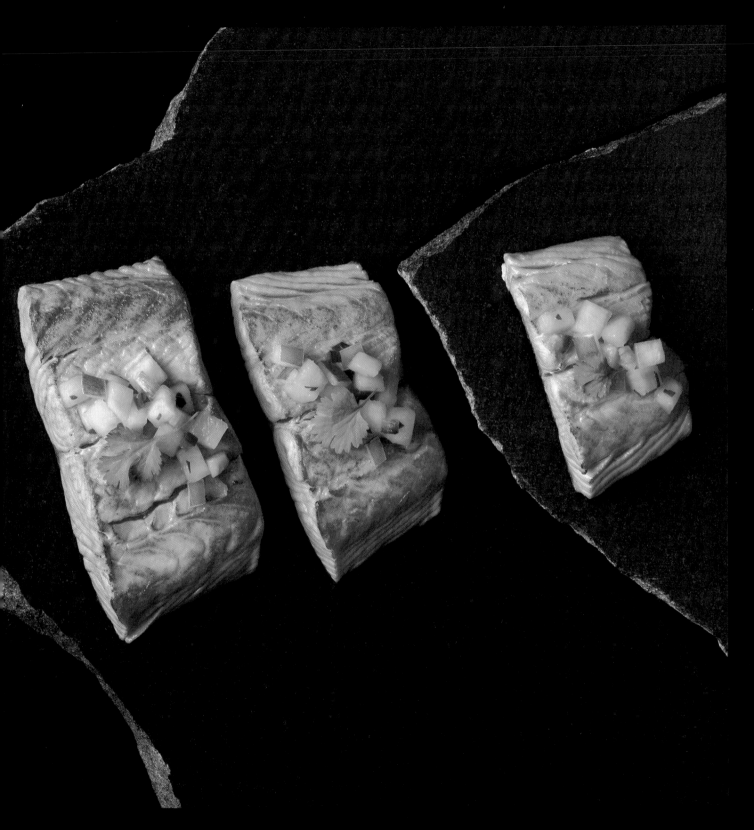

Salmoriglio Villa d' Este

SERVES 4

2 tablespoons dried oregano
2 teaspoons finely minced garlic
1/4 cup virgin olive oil
3 tablespoons fresh lemon juice
2 tablespoons chopped fresh parsley
1/2 teaspoon salt
1/2 teaspoon freshly ground pepper
1/2 cup mild olive oil
4 (6-ounce) fish fillets

Process the oregano and garlic in a blender until puréed. Add 1/4 cup olive oil gradually, processing constantly until the mixture is of the consistency of a paste. Add the lemon juice, parsley, salt and pepper. Process until mixed. Add 1/2 cup olive oil gradually, processing constantly until blended.

Arrange the fillets in a single layer in a shallow nonreactive dish. Pour half the olive oil mixture over the fillets, turning to coat. Marinate, covered, in the refrigerator for 1 to 2 hours, turning occasionally. Bake, grill or broil just until cooked through. Drizzle with the remaining olive oil mixture just before serving.

Note: This is a classic Italian sauce served in many upscale restaurants in Europe. The sauce can also be used as a marinade for pork loin.

Grouper Piccata

SERVES 4

2 pounds Florida black grouper or Florida scamp
1 1/2 cups milk
3/4 cup flour
1 teaspoon seasoned salt
2 tablespoons light olive oil
1 tablespoon butter
1 tablespoon virgin olive oil
1 tablespoon (heaping) Dijon mustard
1/2 cup white chardonnay
Juice of 1 lemon
3/4 cup canned chicken broth
3 tablespoons drained capers

Cut the grouper into 3×4-inch pieces. Arrange in a 9×13-inch glass dish. Pour the milk over the grouper. Marinate, covered, in the refrigerator for 1 hour. Drain and pat dry.

Coat the grouper with the flour and sprinkle with the seasoned salt. Heat 2 tablespoons olive oil in a skillet over medium-high heat. Add the grouper. Cook for 4 minutes per side or until light brown and flaky, turning once; drain. Transfer to a platter. Cover to keep warm.

Heat the butter and 1 tablespoon olive oil in a skillet over medium heat. Add the Dijon mustard. Cook for 30 seconds, stirring constantly. Stir in the wine, lemon juice, broth and capers. Cook for 1 to 2 minutes or until slightly thickened, stirring constantly. Return the grouper to the skillet and spoon the sauce over the fish; reduce the heat.

Simmer for 1 to 2 minutes or just until heated through. Do not cook longer or the sauce will start to separate. Transfer the grouper to a serving platter. Drizzle with the sauce. Garnish with lemon slices and sprigs of parsley. Serve immediately.

Note: Use only Florida scamp or Florida black grouper for this recipe since certain types of grouper yield fillets that are too thin for this recipe.

Boiled Pike "Poor Man's Lobster"

SERVES 4

4 white potatoes
4 red potatoes
4 onions
5 quarts water
1 cup salt
4 large pike fillets
Melted butter

Tie the white potatoes, red potatoes and onions separately in cheesecloth and secure with kitchen twine. Bring the water to a boil in a stockpot. Add the white potatoes and red potatoes. Bring to a boil. Add the salt and onions. Boil for 18 minutes.

Wrap the fillets in cheesecloth and secure with kitchen twine. Add to the stockpot. Return to a boil. Boil for 12 minutes; drain. Discard the cheesecloth and arrange the pike, potatoes and onions on a serving platter. Serve with melted butter.

Note: The ingredients can be decreased or increased according to the number of guests being served.

Salmon Catalan

SERVES 6

1 cup sliced almonds
1 cup olive oil
$^1/2$ cup fresh orange juice
$^1/4$ cup sherry wine vinegar
2 to 3 tablespoons grated orange zest
2 tablespoons drained rinsed capers, chopped
1 tablespoon puréed or finely chopped anchovies
Salt and freshly ground pepper to taste
6 (6-ounce) salmon fillets
Olive oil
3 avocados, sliced

Preheat the oven to 350 degrees. Spread the almonds on a nonstick baking sheet. Toast for 7 minutes or until light brown, stirring occasionally. Let stand until cool and coarsely chop. Whisk 1 cup olive oil, orange juice, wine vinegar, orange zest, capers and anchovies in a bowl. Stir in the almonds. Season with salt and pepper.

Preheat the grill or broiler. Brush the salmon with olive oil. Sprinkle with salt and pepper. Grill or broil for 3 to 4 minutes per side or just until the center is cooked through. Transfer to a serving platter. Arrange the avocado slices around the salmon. Drizzle with the orange sauce.

Note: May bake the salmon at 450 degrees for 8 minutes or until cooked through.

Thai Curried Salmon

SERVES 4

Rice
1¹/₂ cups water
2 tablespoons unsalted butter
1 cup basmati rice

Coconut Sauce
1¹/₈ teaspoons minced gingerroot
1¹/₈ teaspoons minced garlic
2¹/₄ teaspoons peanut oil
1¹/₂ teaspoons curry powder
1¹/₂ teaspoons paprika
1¹/₂ teaspoons Thai red curry paste
³/₄ teaspoon ground coriander seeds
³/₄ teaspoon cumin
1¹/₄ cups unsweetened coconut milk, stirred
3 tablespoons tomato purée
1¹/₂ tablespoons dark brown sugar
1 tablespoon soy sauce

Vegetables and Salmon
3 cups finely shredded green cabbage
³/₄ cup julienned seeded peeled cucumber
3 tablespoons chopped fresh cilantro
3 tablespoons finely chopped fresh mint
3 tablespoons unseasoned rice vinegar
1 tablespoon soy sauce
4 (6-ounce) salmon fillets
Olive oil
Salt and pepper to taste

Assembly
¹/₄ cup roasted peanuts, coarsely chopped

For the rice, combine the water, butter and rice in a saucepan. Cook using package directions.

For the sauce, sauté the gingerroot and garlic in the peanut oil in a skillet over medium-high heat until golden brown. Stir in the curry powder, paprika, red curry paste, ground coriander and cumin. Sauté for 1 minute or until fragrant. Whisk in the coconut milk, tomato purée, brown sugar and soy sauce. Bring just to a boil, stirring frequently. Remove from heat. Cover to keep warm. May be prepared up to 1 day in advance and stored, covered, in the refrigerator. Reheat before serving.

For the vegetables and salmon, toss the cabbage, cucumber, cilantro and mint in a bowl. Add a mixture of the rice vinegar and soy sauce and mix well. Preheat the grill. Brush the salmon with olive oil. Sprinkle with salt and pepper. Place a sheet of foil brushed with oil on the grill rack 5 to 6 inches from the hot coals. Arrange the salmon on the foil. Grill for 5 minutes per side or just until cooked through.

To assemble, spoon equal portions of the rice in the center of each of 4 plates. Arrange the salmon over the rice. Top with the vegetable mixture. Sprinkle with some of the peanuts. Spoon some of the sauce around the outer edge of the rice. Serve immediately with the remaining sauce and remaining peanuts.

Pignoli-Crusted Salmon

SERVES 4

1/2 cup fresh bread crumbs
1/2 cup chopped pine nuts
4 (6-ounce) salmon fillets
2 tablespoons Dijon mustard
1 tablespoon butter
1 teaspoon vegetable oil
2 tablespoons fresh lemon juice
1/4 cup heavy cream
1/4 cup (1/2 stick) butter, chopped, chilled
1/8 teaspoon salt
1/8 teaspoon freshly ground pepper

Preheat the oven to 250 degrees. Spread the bread crumbs on a nonstick baking sheet. Bake for 10 minutes, stirring occasionally. Increase the oven temperature to 350 degrees.

Toss the bread crumbs with the pine nuts in a bowl. Brush the salmon with the Dijon mustard. Pat the crumb mixture on 1 side of each fillet. Heat 1 tablespoon butter and oil in an ovenproof skillet over medium-high heat until the mixture foams. Add the salmon crumb side down. Cook for 3 to 5 minutes or until golden brown; turn. Bake in the oven for 7 to 10 minutes or until the salmon flakes easily with a fork. Remove from oven. Cover to keep warm.

Cook the lemon juice in a saucepan until reduced to 1 teaspoon. Whisk in the heavy cream. Bring to a boil. Boil for 3 minutes or until slightly thickened, stirring frequently. Whisk in 1/4 cup butter until smooth. Stir in the salt and pepper. Serve with the salmon.

Salmon with Pineapple Salsa

SERVES 4

Pineapple Salsa
1 ripe mango, peeled, cut into 1/2-inch cubes
1 cup finely chopped sweet onion
1 cup (1/2-inch) cubes fresh pineapple
1/4 cup chopped fresh cilantro
3 ounces fresh green chiles, minced
3 dashes of Tabasco sauce
Salmon
1 (2-pound) center-cut salmon fillet with skin
2 tablespoons olive oil or vegetable oil
2 tablespoons fresh lemon juice
Salt and freshly ground pepper to taste

For the salsa, combine the mango, onion, pineapple, cilantro, chiles and Tabasco sauce in a bowl and mix gently. Chill, covered, in the refrigerator for up to 3 days.

For the salmon, rinse with cold water and pat dry. Rub both sides of the fillet with the olive oil and lemon juice. Arrange in a dish. Marinate in the refrigerator for 20 to 30 minutes.

Preheat the grill. Place the fillet skin side up on the grill rack. Grill over hot coals for 5 to 7 minutes per side or until the salmon flakes easily, turning once. Remove to a serving platter. Season with salt and pepper. Garnish with sprigs of cilantro. Serve with the salsa.

This sumptuous display of exotic foods is the work of one of Holland's greatest still life painters at the top of his form. In addition to the lobster, the rare fruits and elegant vessels of glass and precious metals send a moralizing message to the would-be diner: beware of the material pleasures of life.

Jan Davidsz de Heem
Dutch, 1606–1684

STILL LIFE WITH A LOBSTER
Oil on canvas, late 1640s

Purchased with funds from the Libbey Endowment, Gift of Edward Drummond Libbey

Sea Bass with Salsa Verde

SERVES 8

Salsa Verde
3/4 cup mild olive oil
1/2 cup fresh orange juice
6 tablespoons fresh lemon juice
1/3 cup minced onion
1 cup chopped fresh mint or basil, or a combination
3 tablespoons grated orange zest
1/2 teaspoon salt
Sea Bass
8 (6-ounce) sea bass, salmon or tuna fillets

For the salsa, whisk the olive oil, orange juice and lemon juice in a bowl until blended. Stir in the onion, mint, orange zest and salt. May prepare up to 1 day in advance and store, covered, in the refrigerator. Bring to room temperature and stir before serving.

For the sea bass, bake, grill, broil or poach until the fish flakes easily. Transfer to serving plates. Top each fillet with some of the salsa and garnish with orange sections.

Note: Salsa Verde is a classic Italian green sauce for fish, meat or vegetables. For variety, drizzle over steamed shrimp or scallops or cooked artichokes, asparagus or green beans.

Sesame-Crusted Sea Bass

SERVES 6

6 tablespoons corn oil
$1/3$ cup soy sauce
3 green onions, chopped
2 tablespoons sugar
1 tablespoon Dijon mustard
2 garlic cloves, crushed
$1/4$ teaspoon white pepper
6 sea bass fillets
$1/2$ to 1 cup sesame seeds

Whisk the corn oil, soy sauce, green onions, sugar, Dijon mustard, garlic and white pepper in a bowl. Pour over the fish in a large sealable plastic bag and seal tightly. Marinate in the refrigerator for 6 to 8 hours, turning occasionally.

Drain the fish, discarding the marinade. Coat with the sesame seeds. Grill over hot coals for 6 to 7 minutes per side or until the fish flakes easily. Transfer to a serving platter.

Serve with a mixture of chopped mango, chopped tomatoes, chopped avocados, chopped garlic and cayenne pepper or commercially prepared mango salsa.

Sole Fillets in White Wine Sauce

SERVES 6

6 sole fillets
1 cup water or fish stock
$1/2$ cup dry white wine
3 tablespoons butter
2 shallots, chopped, or 1 small onion, chopped
Salt and pepper to taste
$1/2$ cup cream
1 tablespoon flour
3 tablespoons butter, chopped

Cut the fillets lengthwise into halves. Roll each half and secure with wooden picks. Arrange the rolls seam side down in a skillet. Stir in the water, white wine, 3 tablespoons butter, shallots, salt and pepper. Bring to a boil; reduce heat.

Simmer for 12 to 15 minutes or until the sole turns white in the center and flakes easily. Remove the fillets with a slotted spoon to a serving platter, reserving the pan juices. Cover the sole to keep warm.

Cook the reserved pan juices until reduced by $2/3$. Stir in a mixture of the cream and flour. Add 3 tablespoons butter. Cook until smooth and slightly thickened, stirring constantly. Drizzle over the sole. Garnish with lemon slices and sprigs of dillweed.

Swordfish Orientale

SERVES 6

2 garlic cloves
1 (3-inch) piece gingerroot, peeled, chopped
3 tablespoons soy sauce
1¹/2 tablespoons hot mustard
¹/3 cup rice vinegar or white wine vinegar
²/3 cup peanut oil
¹/4 cup sesame oil
6 (6-ounce) swordfish or tuna fillets, ³/4 to 1 inch thick
Peanut oil
Salt and freshly ground pepper to taste
¹/2 cup chopped green onions
¹/4 cup chopped fresh cilantro
3 tablespoons sesame seeds, toasted

Combine the garlic, gingerroot, soy sauce and hot mustard in a food processor or blender container. Add the wine vinegar, processing constantly until blended. Add ²/3 cup peanut oil and the sesame oil 1 drop at a time at first and then more quickly until all of the oil has been added and the sauce is emulsified, processing constantly.

Preheat the grill or broiler. Brush the fillets with peanut oil. Sprinkle with salt and pepper. Grill or broil for 3 to 4 minutes per side or until the fish flakes easily. Transfer the fillets to serving plates. Drizzle with the sauce. Sprinkle with the green onions, cilantro and sesame seeds.

Note: May substitute a mixture of 1¹/2 tablespoons Dijon mustard and 1 tablespoon sugar for the hot mustard.

Nipon Tuna

SERVES 6

Juice of 6 limes
¹/2 cup plus 2 tablespoons soy sauce
²/3 cup extra-virgin olive oil
1 tablespoon minced gingerroot
Salt and freshly ground pepper to taste
12 ounces sashimi-grade yellowfin tuna, 1 inch thick
3 cups radish sprouts, arugula or watercress
2 avocados, thinly sliced
1 cup chopped Vidalia or Walla Walla onion
1 tablespoon golden caviar (optional)

Whisk the lime juice, soy sauce, olive oil and gingerroot in a nonmetallic bowl. Season with salt and pepper. Reserve half the lime juice mixture. Cut the tuna into ¹/4-inch slices. Combine the tuna with the remaining lime juice mixture in a bowl and toss gently. Marinate at room temperature while proceeding with the recipe.

Arrange the sprouts on 1 side of each of 6 chilled serving plates. Fan an equal number of avocado slices opposite the sprouts on each plate. Drain the tuna. Arrange the sliced tuna in the center of the plates. Sprinkle with the onion. Top each with ¹/2 teaspoon caviar. Drizzle the reserved lime juice mixture over the tuna and avocado. Serve immediately.

Note: To decrease the raw taste of the tuna, marinate in the refrigerator for 6 to 8 hours.

*S*hrimp Annice—
A masterpiece of simplicity

Late Night Soirée

Pretty Pepper Party Soup

Shrimp Annice

Oriental Cold Asparagus

Tuscan Corn Bread

Frozen Grand Marnier
Soufflé

Wines: Sauvignon Blanc,
New Zealand

Pan-Seared Tuna with Ginger Shiitake Sauce

SERVES 10

10 (6-ounce) tuna steaks, 1 inch thick
Pepper to taste
1/4 cup peanut oil
6 tablespoons butter
2/3 cup chopped green onions
1/2 cup chopped fresh cilantro
1/4 cup finely chopped gingerroot
8 garlic cloves, chopped
1 pound shiitake mushrooms, stems removed, sliced
2 tablespoons soy sauce
3 cups whipping cream
6 tablespoons fresh lime juice

Preheat the oven to 200 degrees. Sprinkle 1 side of each steak with pepper. Heat the peanut oil in a large skillet over high heat. Arrange the steaks pepper side down in the hot oil. Sear for 2 minutes. Cook for 2 minutes longer for rare or until of the desired degree of doneness, turning once. Remove the steaks with a slotted spoon to a baking sheet, reserving the pan drippings. Keep the steaks warm in the oven.

Add the butter, green onions, cilantro, gingerroot and garlic to the reserved pan drippings and mix well. Sauté for 1 minute; reduce the heat. Stir in the mushrooms and soy sauce. Simmer for 1 minute, stirring frequently. Add the whipping cream and mix well.

Simmer for 3 minutes or until the sauce lightly coats the back of a spoon, stirring frequently. Stir in the lime juice. Puddle some of the sauce on each of 10 plates. Arrange the steaks over the sauce. Garnish with lime wedges and sprigs of cilantro. Serve immediately.

Rainbow Trout with Walnuts and Fresh Oregano

SERVES 4

4 teaspoons olive oil
4 teaspoons finely chopped shallots
4 (6-ounce) butterflied rainbow trout fillets
1/4 cup each chopped walnuts and chopped green onions
4 teaspoons finely chopped fresh oregano

Heat the olive oil and shallots in a large skillet until bubbly, stirring frequently. Arrange the fillets flesh side down over the shallots. Sauté for 4 minutes; turn. Cook for 1 minute longer or until the trout flakes easily. Cover to keep warm.

Sauté the walnuts, green onions and oregano in a nonstick skillet for 2 minutes, stirring constantly. Spoon over the trout. Garnish with tomato flowers and sprigs of oregano. Serve immediately.

Pan-Fried Walleye

SERVES 4

1 cup flour
2 eggs
2 tablespoons water
4 walleye pike, perch or bass fillets
Saltines, crushed
Vegetable oil for frying

Pour the flour into a sealable plastic bag. Whisk the eggs and water in a bowl until blended. Add the fillets to the flour and shake to coat. Dip in the egg mixture and coat with the cracker crumbs. Arrange the fillets in a single layer on a baking sheet. Chill, covered, for 1 to 2 hours.

Heat the oil in a cast-iron skillet. Fry the fillets in batches in the hot oil for 2 minutes per side; drain. Arrange on a baking sheet. Keep warm in a 200-degree oven. The secret to success for this recipe is cook the fillets fast, not long.

Pistachio-Encrusted Walleye with Lime Chili Tartar Sauce

SERVES 4 TO 6

Lime Chili Tartar Sauce
1 cup mayonnaise
2 tablespoons chopped fresh cilantro
2 tablespoons chopped sweet pickle relish
Juice of 1 lime
1 tablespoon chili powder
1 tablespoon cumin
3 dashes of hot pepper sauce
Salt and pepper to taste
Walleye
1 cup finely chopped pistachios
3/4 cup unseasoned bread crumbs
2 eggs
1/2 cup milk
1 to 1 1/2 pounds walleye pike fillets
Olive oil
Salt and pepper to taste

For the sauce, combine the mayonnaise, cilantro, pickle relish, lime juice, chili powder, cumin, hot pepper sauce, salt and pepper in a bowl and mix well. Chill, covered, until serving time.

For the walleye, preheat the oven to 425 degrees. Combine the pistachios and bread crumbs in a shallow dish and mix well. Whisk the eggs and milk in a bowl until blended. Dip the fillets into the egg mixture and coat with the bread crumb mixture.

Arrange the fillets in a single layer on a greased baking sheet. Drizzle with olive oil. Sprinkle with salt and pepper. Bake for 12 to 15 minutes or until the fillets flake easily with a fork; do not overcook. Spoon the sauce over the fillets or serve on the side.

Lemon Basil Whitefish

SERVES 8

4 pounds whitefish fillets
1/2 cup (1 stick) butter, melted
3 tablespoons lemon juice
3 tablespoons chopped fresh basil
1/2 teaspoon salt
1/2 teaspoon pepper
1/2 teaspoon paprika
1 lemon, thinly sliced
1 tablespoon chopped fresh parsley

Preheat the oven to 325 degrees. Arrange the fillets in a single layer in two 9×13-inch baking dishes. Drizzle with the butter and lemon juice. Sprinkle with the basil, salt, pepper and paprika.

Bake for 20 to 25 minutes or until the fillets flake easily with a fork, basting frequently with the pan juices; do not allow to dry out. Transfer the fillets to a serving platter. Top with the lemon slices and sprinkle with the parsley.

Sautéed Whitefish with Sun-Dried Tomato-Basil Mayonnaise

SERVES 4

Sun-Dried Tomato-Basil Mayonnaise
3/4 cup mayonnaise
8 oil-pack sun-dried tomatoes, finely chopped
2 to 3 tablespoons chopped fresh basil
1 tablespoon lemon juice
1 teaspoon minced garlic
Salt and pepper to taste
Whitefish
1 cup flour
Salt and pepper to taste
4 (8-ounce) whitefish or cod fillets
1 cup peanut or vegetable oil

For the mayonnaise, combine the mayonnaise, sun-dried tomatoes, basil, lemon juice, garlic, salt and pepper in a bowl and mix well. Chill, covered, in the refrigerator.

For the whitefish, mix the flour, salt and pepper in a shallow dish. Coat the fillets lightly with the flour mixture. Heat the peanut oil in a skillet over medium heat. Fry the fish in the hot oil until golden brown on each side; drain. Serve with the mayonnaise.

Lobster Newburg

SERVES 4 TO 6

1/2 cup (1 stick) butter
1 1/2 pounds cooked lobster meat, shrimp or crab meat, chopped
4 ounces brandy
1 tablespoon paprika
5 ounces sherry
1 tablespoon butter
1 tablespoon flour
1 cup half-and-half
1 cup heavy cream
1 teaspoon salt
1/8 teaspoon white pepper
1 tablespoon chilled butter

Heat 1/2 cup butter in a skillet until melted. Stir in the lobster meat. Cook for 5 minutes, stirring frequently. Add the brandy and paprika and mix well. Cook until heated through, stirring frequently; flame. Add the sherry and flame again.

Heat 1 tablespoon butter in a saucepan until melted. Add the flour, whisking until smooth. Cook until bubbly, stirring constantly; do not brown. Stir into the lobster mixture with the half-and-half and heavy cream. Add the salt and white pepper and mix well.

Cook until of the desired consistency, stirring constantly; do not allow to boil. Whisk in 1 tablespoon chilled butter. Spoon over toast points or into puff pastry shells. Serve immediately.

Note: Fresh cooked lobster meat can be found at some fish markets or supermarkets.

Scalloped Oysters

SERVES 2 TO 4

1 quart oysters
3 cups cracker crumbs
2 cups milk
2/3 cup butter
1 teaspoon salt
1/4 teaspoon Worcestershire sauce
2 eggs, beaten

Preheat the oven to 350 degrees. Drain the oysters, reserving the liquor. Line the bottom of a 1 1/2-quart baking dish with some of the cracker crumbs. Layer the oysters and remaining cracker crumbs alternately in the prepared dish until all of the ingredients are used.

Heat the milk, butter, salt, Worcestershire sauce and some of the reserved oyster liquor in a saucepan until hot, stirring occasionally. Stir a small amount of the hot milk mixture into the eggs. Stir the egg mixture into the hot milk mixture. Pour over the prepared layers. Bake for 1 hour.

T his magnificent basin is a masterpiece of the trompe l'oeil, or "fool the eye" aesthetic. When filled with water, its richly colored aquatic creatures and plant forms seem to come to life.

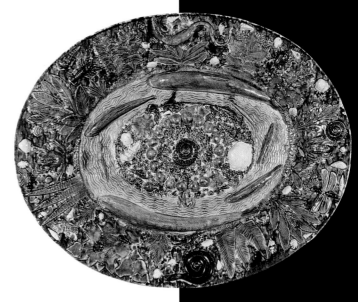

Style of Bernard Palissy
French, about 1510–1590

OVAL BASIN
Glazed earthenware,
late 16th century

Gift of
Mr. and Mrs. Marvin Kobacker

Scallops Provençale

SERVES 4 TO 6

2 tablespoons olive oil
4 green onions with tops, chopped
2 garlic cloves, minced
1 (16-ounce) can tomatoes
1/2 cup dry white wine
2 tablespoons chopped fresh basil, or 2 teaspoons dried basil
2 tablespoons tomato paste
1/2 teaspoon salt
1/8 teaspoon red pepper flakes
1 pound bay scallops, drained, rinsed
1 (14-ounce) can artichoke hearts, drained, cut into quarters
8 ounces linguini, cooked, drained
Grated Parmesan cheese to taste
2 tablespoons slivered almonds, toasted

Heat the olive oil in a skillet. Add the green onions and garlic. Cook until the green onions are tender, stirring frequently. Add the undrained tomatoes, white wine, basil, tomato paste, salt and red pepper flakes, stirring until the tomatoes are broken into chunks. Bring to a boil; reduce heat.

Simmer, covered, for 20 minutes, stirring occasionally. Add the scallops and artichokes and mix well. Cook for 5 minutes or until the scallops are tender, stirring frequently. Add the pasta and toss to mix. Add the desired amount of cheese and mix well. Spoon into a serving bowl. Sprinkle with the almonds. Serve immediately.

El Greco's Shrimp

SERVES 4

1/2 cup minced onion
1 1/2 tablespoons butter
1 1/2 tablespoons olive oil
4 medium ripe tomatoes, peeled, seeded, chopped
1/2 cup dry white wine
1 small garlic clove, minced
1 teaspoon salt
3/4 teaspoon oregano
1/4 teaspoon freshly ground pepper
4 ounces feta cheese, crumbled
1 pound large shrimp, peeled, deveined, drained
1/4 cup chopped fresh parsley

Sauté the onion in a mixture of the butter and olive oil in a skillet until tender. Stir in the tomatoes, white wine, garlic, salt, oregano and pepper. Bring to a boil; reduce heat.

Simmer until slightly thickened, stirring constantly. Stir in the cheese. Simmer for 10 to 15 minutes longer or until of the desired consistency, stirring frequently. Adjust the seasonings. Add the shrimp and mix well.

Cook for 5 minutes or until the shrimp turn pink, stirring frequently; do not overcook. Spoon into bowls. Sprinkle with the parsley. Serve immediately with crusty French bread.

Note: May prepare up to 6 to 8 hours in advance and store, covered, in the refrigerator. Reheat the sauce and add the shrimp just before serving.

Shrimp Annice

SERVES 10 TO 12

2 (6-ounce) packages chicken-flavor long grain and wild rice
4 pounds fresh or frozen shrimp, peeled, deveined
2¹/2 cups small fresh whole mushrooms
2¹/2 cups black olives
2¹/2 cups sliced pimentos
2¹/2 cups chopped onions
2¹/2 cups chopped green bell peppers
Butter
3 (6-ounce) jars marinated artichoke hearts

Cook the rice using package directions. Sauté the shrimp, mushrooms, olives, pimentos, onions and bell peppers separately in butter in a skillet until the vegetables are tender and the shrimp turn pink.

Combine the rice, shrimp, mushrooms, olives, pimentos, onions and bell peppers in a large saucepan and mix well. Stir in the undrained artichokes. Cook over low heat just until heated through, stirring frequently. Spoon into a serving bowl. Garnish with whole cooked shrimp.

Note: May substitute 1 cup uncooked wild rice for the chicken-flavor long grain and wild rice.

Elegant Party Casserole

SERVES 18 TO 20

3 pounds fresh mushrooms, thickly sliced
2 to 4 tablespoons butter
8 whole chicken breasts, cooked, coarsely chopped
2 pounds deveined peeled cooked shrimp
3 (14-ounce) cans artichoke hearts, drained, cut into quarters
³/4 cup (1¹/2 sticks) butter
²/3 cup flour
1 tablespoon salt
1¹/2 teaspoons pepper
6 cups milk
1 cup sherry or white wine
2 tablespoons Worcestershire sauce
¹/2 cup freshly grated Parmesan cheese

Heat 2 to 4 tablespoons butter in a skillet. Sauté the mushrooms in the butter until tender. Layer equal amounts of the chicken, shrimp, mushrooms and artichokes in 2 greased 9×13-inch baking dishes.

Preheat the oven to 375 degrees. Heat ³/4 cup butter in a saucepan over low heat until melted. Add the flour, salt and pepper and stir until blended. Cook over low heat until bubbly and smooth, stirring constantly. Remove from heat. Add the milk gradually, stirring constantly. Bring to a boil, stirring constantly. Boil for 1 minute, stirring constantly. Stir in the sherry and Worcestershire sauce. Pour over the prepared layers. Sprinkle with the cheese. Bake for 45 minutes.

*The recipes featured here
are Fillet de Boeuf Roulade
and Roast Duck with Peaches,
Almonds and Ginger.*

Pepper-Coated Roast Beef with Red Pepper Basil Butter

SERVES 12

Roast Beef
1 (4-pound) eye of round roast
$1/3$ cup Dijon mustard
3 tablespoons coarsely ground black peppercorns
Red Pepper Basil Butter
1 (7-ounce) jar roasted red peppers, drained
$3/4$ cup ($1^1/2$ sticks) butter, softened
3 tablespoons minced fresh basil, or 2 teaspoons dried basil
3 tablespoons minced fresh parsley

For the beef, let the roast stand at room temperature for 15 minutes. Preheat the oven to 425 degrees. Rub the surface of the roast with the Dijon mustard. Sprinkle the peppercorns evenly over the roast. Place on a rack in a baking pan. Bake, loosely covered with foil, for 45 to 55 minutes or until a meat thermometer inserted in the center of the roast registers 145 degrees. Remove the roast to a serving platter.

For the butter, rinse the red peppers and pat dry with paper towels; finely mince. Beat the butter in a mixing bowl until fluffy. Stir in the red peppers, basil and parsley. You may prepare up to 1 day in advance and store, covered, in the refrigerator.

To serve, cut the roast across the grain into thin slices. Serve with the butter.

Note: Roasted hot or sweet peppers may be prepared following these instructions. Preheat the broiler. Place the peppers 2 inches from the heat source and roast for 2 to 3 minutes or until blackened and blistered on all sides, turning frequently. Place the peppers in a nonrecycled paper bag and seal tightly. Let stand until cool. The steam that builds up inside the bag will loosen the skins of the peppers so they can be peeled. After peeling, proceed to seed and chop according to recipe instructions.

Lemon Lime Grilled Tenderloin

SERVES 6

$1/2$ cup packed light brown sugar
6 tablespoons olive oil
$1/4$ cup red wine vinegar
Juice of 1 lime
Juice of $1/2$ lemon
3 tablespoons whole grain mustard
3 medium garlic cloves, minced
$1^1/2$ teaspoons salt
1 (3-pound) beef tenderloin, trimmed

Combine the brown sugar, olive oil, wine vinegar, lime juice, lemon juice, mustard, garlic and salt in a bowl and mix well. Pour over the beef in a shallow 9×13-inch dish and turn to coat. Marinate, covered, in the refrigerator for 3 hours. Let stand at room temperature for 1 hour.

Preheat the grill to 400 degrees. Grill for 20 minutes per side for medium or until of the desired degree of doneness. Let rest for 5 minutes. Cut into $1/2$- to $3/4$-inch slices and arrange on a serving platter. Garnish with fresh basil and/or edible flowers.

Note: Use this marinade with chicken breasts and pork tenderloin. Marinate the chicken in the refrigerator for 8 to 10 hours and marinate the pork following the instructions for the beef.

Filet de Boeuf Roulade

SERVES 6

1¹/4 pounds fresh spinach, trimmed
8 ounces Montrachet cheese, crumbled
1 teaspoon dried rosemary, crushed
1 teaspoon dried thyme
¹/2 teaspoon each salt and freshly ground pepper
1 (3-pound) beef filet, trimmed
Salt and pepper to taste
3 medium red bell peppers, roasted, peeled, cut into quarters
2 tablespoons extra-virgin olive oil
8 ounces bacon, blanched

Reserve 8 large spinach leaves. Blanch the remaining spinach in a small amount of water in a saucepan for 2 minutes or just until wilted; drain. Refresh under cold water; drain. Pat dry; coarsely chop.

Combine the spinach, cheese, rosemary, thyme, ¹/2 teaspoon salt and ¹/2 teaspoon pepper in a bowl and mix well. Shape the cheese mixture into a 12-inch log on a sheet of waxed paper. Chill, wrapped in waxed paper, until firm. May prepare the cheese log up to 1 day in advance and store in the refrigerator.

Butterfly the fillet by cutting lengthwise down the center 2/3 of the way through. Open the fillet flat, book-style and place between sheets of waxed paper. Pound ³/4 inch thick with a meat mallet. Season with salt and pepper to taste. Arrange the 8 reserved spinach leaves over the cut side of the beef, leaving a 1-inch border. Layer with the bell peppers peeled side up. Place the cheese log on 1 side of the fillet. Roll the beef into a tight roll, tucking the tail end under. Secure with kitchen twine at 1-inch intervals.

Preheat the oven to 375 degrees. Brown the beef roll in the olive oil in a skillet for 10 minutes or until brown on all sides. Place the beef on a rack in a roasting pan. Arrange the bacon over the top. Roast for 35 minutes or until a meat thermometer registers 125 degrees for rare. Let stand for 15 minutes. Discard the bacon and slice the roll. Garnish with chopped fresh chives.

Boeuf au Fromage

SERVES 2 TO 4

¹/2 cup flour
¹/2 teaspoon salt
¹/4 teaspoon pepper
1 (1-pound) beef tenderloin, cut into ¹/4-inch slices
2 tablespoons peanut oil
2 tablespoons butter
1 cup beef stock
1 tablespoon sour cream
2 tablespoons Roquefort salad dressing
2 tablespoons freshly grated Parmesan cheese

Mix the flour, salt and pepper together. Coat the tenderloin with the flour mixture, shaking off the excess. Heat the peanut oil and butter in a skillet. Sauté the beef in batches in the hot peanut oil mixture until brown on both sides. Remove the beef to a platter with a slotted spoon, reserving the pan drippings. Reduce the heat to low.

Stir the stock and sour cream into the reserved pan drippings. Return the beef to the skillet and stir gently. Remove from heat.

Preheat the broiler. Spoon the beef and sauce into a greased baking dish. Top with the salad dressing and sprinkle with the cheese. Broil until light brown. Serve immediately.

Marinated Sirloin

SERVES 8

1 cup pineapple juice
1 small bottle soy sauce
1/2 cup bourbon or brandy
1/4 cup vinegar
3 garlic cloves, crushed
1 teaspoon meat tenderizer
1 teaspoon Worcestershire sauce
1 sirloin steak, 2 inches thick

Combine the pineapple juice, soy sauce, bourbon, vinegar, garlic, Worcestershire sauce and meat tenderizer in a bowl and mix well. Pour over the steak in a shallow dish and turn to coat. Marinate, covered, in the refrigerator for 2 to 10 hours, occasionally.

Preheat the grill. Drain the steak, discarding the marinade. Grill the steak over hot coals for 10 to 12 minutes per side or until of the desired degree of doneness, turning once. Remove to a platter. Cut the steak diagonally into thin slices.

Cranberry Brisket

SERVES 8

1 (3- to 4-pound) flat-cut beef brisket
Salt and pepper to taste
2 to 3 tablespoons olive oil
1 (16-ounce) can whole-berry cranberry sauce
1/2 cup packed brown sugar
1/4 cup sherry
1 envelope onion soup mix
2 tablespoons tomato paste

Sprinkle both sides of the brisket with salt and pepper. Heat the olive oil in a medium roasting pan until hot. Add the brisket. Cook until brown on both sides. Remove from heat.

Preheat the oven to 300 degrees. Combine the cranberry sauce, brown sugar, sherry, soup mix and tomato paste in a bowl and mix well. Pour over the brisket and turn to coat. Bake, covered, for 2 1/2 to 3 hours or until cooked through.

Note: May remove the brisket to a platter and cut into 1/2-inch slices with an electric knife 45 minutes before the end of the baking process. Holding the slices together, return the brisket to the roasting pan along with potatoes, carrots and onions if desired. Bake until the brisket is cooked through and the vegetables are tender. May prepare up to 1 day in advance and store, covered, in the refrigerator. Reheat before serving.

Flank Steak with Pistachio Herb Stuffing

SERVES 6

1 (2-pound) beef flank steak
1/2 large onion, chopped
1 garlic clove, minced
2 tablespoons butter
1/2 cup chopped mushrooms
1 1/2 cups soft bread cubes
1/4 cup coarsely chopped pistachios
1/4 cup chopped fresh parsley
1 egg, lightly beaten
3/4 teaspoon oregano-basil mixture
1/2 teaspoon salt
Freshly ground pepper to taste
1 to 2 tablespoons butter
1/2 cup water, dry wine or bouillon

Preheat the oven to 350 degrees. Pound the steak on a hard surface with a meat mallet or score lightly on both sides. Sauté the onion and garlic in 2 tablespoons butter in a skillet until light brown. Add the mushrooms and mix well. Cook for 3 minutes, stirring frequently. Stir in the bread cubes, pistachios, parsley, egg, oregano mixture, salt and pepper and mix well.

Spread the bread cube mixture over the surface of 1 side of the steak. Roll as for a jelly roll. Secure the roll with kitchen twine at 2-inch intervals. Brown the roll in 1 to 2 tablespoons butter in an ovenproof skillet. Stir in the water.

Bake, covered, for 2 hours. Remove the roll to a platter. Cut into 1-inch slices. Serve with the pan drippings.

Flank Steak Stir-Fry

SERVES 2 OR 3

8 ounces fresh green beans
2 tablespoons soy sauce
1 tablespoon cornstarch
1 tablespoon sherry
1 teaspoon sugar
1/2 to 1 teaspoon salt, or to taste
8 ounces beef flank steak, thinly sliced,
*   cut into 2- to 3-inch pieces*
2 tablespoons olive oil
4 ounces sliced mushrooms

Cook the green beans in a small amount of water in a saucepan until tender-crisp. Drain, reserving 1/4 cup of the liquid. Combine the soy sauce, cornstarch, sherry, sugar and salt in a bowl and mix well. Pour over the beef in a shallow dish, turning to coat. Marinate, covered, in the refrigerator for 1 hour or longer, turning occasionally. Drain the beef, reserving the marinade.

Stir-fry the beef in the olive oil in a wok for several minutes. Add the mushrooms. Stir-fry for several minutes. Add the green beans, reserved liquid and reserved marinade and mix well. Simmer until heated through, stirring frequently; do not overcook. Serve over hot cooked rice.

This rhyton in the shape of a wild boar's head is rendered in a lively and animated fashion. It was not made for drinking or everyday use, but as an offering to be placed in a tomb.

Painter of Louvre 1148
Greek, South Italian, Apulian

BOAR'S HEAD RHYTON
Earthenware, 340–330 B.C.

Purchased with funds from the Libbey Endowment, Gift of Edward Drummond Libbey, and with funds from the Latin Students of Donnell Junior High School, Findlay

Special Filet Mignon

SERVES 8

2 large garlic cloves, finely minced
1 tablespoon seasoned salt
1/2 teaspoon seasoned pepper
8 (8-ounce) filet mignon steaks, 1 1/2 inches thick
1/2 cup (1 stick) butter
2 tablespoons brandy
1/4 cup flour
1 tablespoon tomato paste
2 garlic cloves, finely minced
1 cup each chicken broth, beef broth and red burgundy
1/2 cup water
3 tablespoons currant jelly
1/2 teaspoon Worcestershire sauce

Mix 2 garlic cloves, seasoned salt and seasoned pepper in a bowl until a paste forms. Rub the surface of the steaks with the paste. Sauté the steaks 1 at a time in 2 tablespoons of the butter in a skillet until brown, lifting the skillet off the heat for several seconds if the butter starts to burn. Arrange the steaks in a single layer in a shallow baking dish and place in the refrigerator, returning the dish to the refrigerator after each addition.

Stir the brandy into the pan drippings to deglaze. Add remaining 6 tablespoons butter and heat until bubbly, stirring constantly. Stir in the flour, tomato paste and 2 garlic cloves. Remove from heat. Stir in the chicken broth, beef broth, burgundy and water.

Cook until blended, stirring constantly. Reduce the heat. Cook for 5 minutes, stirring occasionally. Stir in the jelly and Worcestershire sauce. Cook until the jelly dissolves, stirring constantly. Let stand until cool. Pour over the filets, turning to coat.

Marinate, covered, in the refrigerator for 8 to 10 hours, turning occasionally. Bring the steaks to room temperature. Preheat the oven to 400 degrees. Bake for 15 minutes for medium-rare or until of the desired degree of doneness. Garnish with sautéed sliced mushrooms.

Carbonnade à la Flamande

1 beef bouillon cube
1/2 cup boiling water
2 pounds boneless beef chuck or round steak,
    cut into 1-inch cubes
Flour
3 tablespoons vegetable oil
2 tablespoons minced fresh parsley
1 1/2 teaspoons salt
1/2 teaspoon marjoram
1/2 teaspoon thyme
1/2 teaspoon pepper
4 medium onions, sliced
2 garlic cloves, minced
1/3 cup butter
2 tablespoons cornstarch
1 tablespoon brown sugar
6 ounces beer
1 bay leaf

Preheat the oven to 300 degrees. Dissolve the bouillon cube in the boiling water. Coat the beef with flour. Brown the beef in the oil in a skillet; drain. Stir in the parsley, salt, marjoram, thyme and pepper. Spoon the beef mixture into a 3-quart baking dish. Sauté the onions and garlic in the butter in a skillet until the onions are tender. Spoon over the beef mixture.

Combine the cornstarch and brown sugar in a bowl and mix well. Stir in the bouillon, beer and bay leaf. Pour over the prepared layers. Bake, covered, for 2 to 2 1/2 hours or until the beef is cooked through. Discard the bay leaf. Serve over hot cooked noodles seasoned with butter, dillweed, salt and pepper.

Country Beef Stew

8 ounces salt pork, chopped
2 pounds beef stew meat
3/4 cup flour
1 teaspoon salt
1/2 teaspoon pepper
1 bouillon cube
1 cup hot water
1 (8-ounce) can tomato sauce
1/4 cup chopped fresh parsley
1 1/2 garlic cloves, chopped
1 large onion, chopped
10 peppercorns
3 whole cloves
1/2 bay leaf
1/2 cup sherry
6 carrots, peeled, cut into quarters, cooked
6 medium potatoes, cut into quarters, cooked
1 rib celery, chopped, cooked
6 to 8 mushrooms, cooked

Sauté the salt pork in a large skillet. Discard the salt pork, reserving the pan drippings. Coat the beef with a mixture of the flour, salt and pepper. Brown in the reserved pan drippings; drain. Spoon the beef into a heavy saucepan.

Dissolve the bouillon cube in the hot water. Combine the bouillon, tomato sauce, parsley, garlic, onion, peppercorns, cloves and bay leaf in a saucepan. Bring to a boil, stirring occasionally. Pour over the beef and mix well. Simmer, covered, for 3 hours, stirring occasionally. Stir in the sherry. Simmer for 1 hour longer, stirring occasionally. Discard the peppercorns, cloves and bay leaf.

To serve, divide the cooked vegetables equally among 6 to 8 bowls. Spoon the beef mixture over the top. The flavor of the stew is enhanced if prepared 1 day in advance and stored, covered, in the refrigerator. Reheat before serving.

Mushroom-Herb Stuffed Leg of Lamb

SERVES 12 TO 14

1 (5^1/2-pound) leg of lamb
8 ounces ground veal
8 ounces ground cooked ham
^{1}/2 cup fine dry bread crumbs
8 ounces mushrooms, finely chopped
1 egg, lightly beaten
1 tablespoon Worcestershire sauce
1 tablespoon orange marmalade
1 teaspoon salt
^{1}/2 teaspoon oregano
^{1}/4 teaspoon pepper
1 small garlic clove, crushed
Garlic cloves to taste, slivered
2 tablespoons Dijon mustard
1 tablespoon orange marmalade

Have the butcher bone the leg of lamb, leaving approximately 3 inches of the shank so the roast will maintain its original shape. Preheat the oven to 325 degrees.

Combine the ground veal, ground ham, bread crumbs, mushrooms, egg, Worcestershire sauce, 1 tablespoon orange marmalade, salt, oregano, pepper and crushed garlic in a bowl and mix well. Pack the mixture into the lamb leg. Secure the opening with skewers and twine.

Make several slashes in the lamb leg and insert the garlic slivers. Coat the leg with a mixture of the Dijon mustard and 1 tablespoon orange marmalade. Arrange fat side up on a rack in a shallow baking pan. Bake for 30 to 35 minutes per pound. Let rest for 10 minutes before carving.

Rolled Lamb with Artichokes

SERVES 8

1 (5-pound) leg of lamb, boned
1 garlic clove, cut into halves
Salt and pepper to taste
^{2}/3 cup chopped onion
6 tablespoons butter
1 cup coarsely chopped canned artichoke hearts
2 cups fresh bread crumbs
4 teaspoons chopped fresh parsley
^{1}/2 teaspoon salt
^{1}/4 teaspoon thyme
^{1}/4 teaspoon marjoram
^{1}/4 teaspoon dillweed
^{1}/4 teaspoon pepper
3 cups consommé
^{1}/4 cup flour

Preheat the oven to 325 degrees. Rub the lamb with the garlic. Sprinkle with salt and pepper to taste. Sauté the onion in the butter in a skillet until golden brown. Stir in the artichokes. Cook for 2 minutes, stirring frequently. Add the bread crumbs, parsley, ^{1}/2 teaspoon salt, thyme, marjoram, dillweed and ^{1}/4 teaspoon pepper. Pack the mixture into the lamb leg and secure with skewers and twine.

Place the lamb in a roasting pan. Roast for 35 minutes per pound, adding 1 cup of the consommé 20 minutes before the end of the roasting process. Remove the lamb to a heated platter, reserving ^{1}/4 cup of the pan drippings. Cover to keep warm.

Combine the reserved pan drippings and flour in a saucepan and mix until smooth. Stir in the remaining 2 cups consommé. Cook until smooth and thick, stirring constantly. Season with salt and pepper to taste. Serve with the lamb.

Indienne Lamb Curry

SERVES 20

10 pounds boneless lamb, cut into 1-inch cubes
5 (6-ounce) cans tomato paste
5 large onions, chopped
5 to 10 tart apples, grated
5 cups water
1 1/4 cups raisins
1/2 cup plus 2 tablespoons curry powder
10 beef bouillon cubes
5 teaspoons salt
5 teaspoons parsley flakes
5 teaspoons Worcestershire sauce
2 1/2 teaspoons ground ginger
2 1/2 teaspoons coriander
1 teaspoon pepper

Combine the lamb, tomato paste, onions, apples, water, raisins, curry powder, bouillon cubes, salt, parsley flakes, Worcestershire sauce, ginger, coriander and pepper in a large saucepan and mix well. Bring to a simmer, stirring occasionally.

Simmer, covered, for 1 hour or until the lamb is cooked through, stirring occasionally. Serve with hot cooked rice. Garnish with crushed peanuts, shredded coconut and additional raisins.

Roasted Pork Loin with Garlic and Rosemary

SERVES 6 TO 8

10 garlic cloves
1 tablespoon fresh rosemary leaves
2 teaspoons black peppercorns
Salt to taste
2 tablespoons olive oil
1 (3-pound) boneless pork loin roast, butterflied
1/2 to 1 cup water

Preheat the oven to 400 degrees. Process the garlic, rosemary leaves, peppercorns and salt in a food processor until finely chopped. Brush a roasting pan with the olive oil. Spread half the garlic mixture over the pork. Fold over and reshape the pork loin. Secure with twine at 1-inch intervals. Place in the prepared roasting pan. Spread the pork with the remaining garlic mixture.

Roast for 20 to 25 minutes. Pour 1/2 cup water over the pork; turn the pork. Roast for 45 to 60 minutes or until cooked through, turning and adding additional water as needed. Transfer the roast to a cutting board. Let stand for 10 minutes. Discard the twine. Cut into 3/8-inch slices.

Garnish with sprigs of fresh rosemary. Serve warm with risotto and vegetables of your choice during the fall, winter and spring. Serve at room temperature in the summer with fresh tomatoes and Italian potato salad.

Note: May prepare up to 1 day in advance and store, covered, in the refrigerator.

Pork Loin Jubilee

SERVES 8

1 (3-pound) boneless pork loin roast
Salt and pepper to taste
1 (12-ounce) jar cherry preserves
1/4 cup red wine vinegar
2 tablespoons light corn syrup
1/4 teaspoon cinnamon
1/4 teaspoon nutmeg
1/4 teaspoon ground cloves
1/4 cup slivered almonds, toasted

Preheat the oven to 325 degrees. Rub the pork with salt and pepper. Place the pork on a rack in a shallow roasting pan. Roast for 1 1/4 to 1 1/2 hours or 30 to 45 minutes per pound.

Combine the preserves, wine vinegar, corn syrup, cinnamon, nutmeg and cloves in a saucepan and mix well. Bring to a boil, stirring constantly; reduce the heat. Simmer for 2 minutes, stirring occasionally. Stir in the almonds. Spoon some of the sauce over the pork.

Roast for 30 minutes longer or until a meat thermometer registers 170 degrees, basting frequently with the sauce. Remove the pork to a serving platter. Let rest for several minutes before carving. Bring the remaining sauce to a boil, stirring frequently. Serve with the pork.

Pork Tenderloins Stuffed with Apricots and Spinach

SERVES 6

Tenderloin
2 (3/4- to 1-pound) pork tenderloins, butterflied
8 ounces fresh baby spinach leaves
1 cup sliced dried apricots
6 garlic cloves, crushed
2 tablespoons coarse salt
2 tablespoons butter, softened
Apricot Glaze
1 (11-ounce) jar apricot preserves
1/4 cup apricot brandy or orange liqueur
Canned chicken broth (optional)

For the tenderloins, preheat the oven to 350 degrees. Spread the tenderloins flat on a hard surface. Lay the spinach leaves slightly overlapping the length of the tenderloins. Top with the apricots. Fold the tenderloins over to cover the filling. Secure with wooden picks if necessary. Place in a roasting pan.

Combine the garlic, coarse salt and butter in a bowl and stir until the mixture forms a paste. Spread over the tops of the tenderloins. Bake for 40 minutes or until a meat thermometer registers 170 degrees. Remove to a serving platter and slice. Garnish with spiced crabapples or canned apple slices and sprigs of fresh parsley.

For the glaze, combine the preserves and brandy in a blender. Process until puréed. Transfer the mixture to a saucepan. Cook just until heated through, stirring frequently. Add a small amount of chicken broth if the glaze is too sweet. Serve with the pork.

Veal Chops with Pineapple—
A new interpretation

Veal Chops with Pineapple

SERVES 4

$1^1/2$ cups fresh or canned pineapple juice
2 tablespoons julienned peeled gingerroot
2 tablespoons lemon juice
1 tablespoon butter
1 teaspoon bitter orange marmalade
Salt and black pepper to taste
Cayenne pepper to taste
$^1/2$ cup pine nuts, lightly toasted
4 rib veal chops
2 tablespoons extra-virgin olive oil
Minced fresh chives

Combine the pineapple juice and gingerroot in a saucepan. Cook over medium heat for 10 minutes or until reduced by half, stirring occasionally. Stir in the lemon juice, butter, marmalade, salt, black pepper and cayenne pepper. Add additional lemon juice if using sweet marmalade. Taste and adjust the seasonings; the mixture should be quite strong. Add the pine nuts and mix well.

Preheat the oven to 350 degrees. Season the veal chops with salt and black pepper. Pour the olive oil into a large ovenproof skillet. Heat over high heat until hot. Add the chops. Sear on 1 side for 3 minutes; turn. Roast for 10 to 15 minutes or until cooked through, turning once or twice. Transfer to a serving platter. Spoon the pineapple sauce over the top. Sprinkle with chives.

Veal Scaloppine with Gorgonzola

SERVES 4

4 ounces Gorgonzola cheese, softened
$^1/2$ cup coarsely chopped walnuts
2 tablespoons heavy cream
1 tablespoon marsala or madeira
8 veal scaloppine, lightly pounded
$^1/2$ teaspoon salt
$^1/4$ teaspoon freshly ground pepper
1 egg, lightly beaten
2 tablespoons flour
$1^1/2$ cups fresh fine bread crumbs
Vegetable oil

Combine the cheese, walnuts, heavy cream and wine in a bowl and mix well. Sprinkle the veal with the salt and pepper. Spoon $^1/4$ of the cheese mixture onto the center of each of the veal slices. Brush the edges with the egg. Top each with another veal slice and press the edges to seal.

Coat both sides of the veal packets with the flour. Dip in egg. Coat with bread crumbs, pressing lightly so the bread crumbs will adhere. Pour enough oil into a skillet to measure $^1/4$ inch. Heat over medium-high heat until hot. Add the veal. Sauté for 3 minutes per side or until golden brown, turning once. Serve immediately.

Osso Buco

SERVES 8 TO 10

1 1/2 cups finely chopped onions
1 cup each finely chopped carrots and celery
1 garlic clove, finely chopped
2 tablespoons butter
4 pounds veal, cut into 2-inch cubes
Salt and pepper to taste
Flour
Vegetable shortening
1 cup dry white wine
3 cups drained canned tomatoes, finely chopped
1 cup chicken stock
6 sprigs of parsley
2 bay leaves
1/2 teaspoon each thyme and basil
3 tablespoons finely chopped fresh parsley
1 tablespoon grated lemon zest

Cook the onions, carrots, celery and garlic in the butter in a Dutch oven over medium heat until the vegetables are tender, stirring occasionally. Sprinkle the veal with salt and pepper. Coat with flour.

Preheat the oven to 350 degrees. Brown the veal in shortening in a skillet. Transfer the veal with a slotted spoon to the Dutch oven and mix with the vegetables. Drain most of the pan drippings from the skillet. Stir the white wine into the remaining pan drippings. Bring to a boil.

Boil until reduced to about 1/2 cup, stirring to loosen any browned bits. Add the tomatoes, stock, sprigs of parsley, bay leaves, thyme and basil and mix well. Bring to a boil, stirring occasionally. Pour over the veal mixture. Bring to a boil, stirring occasionally.

Bake, covered, for 1 1/2 hours or until the veal is tender, adding additional stock if needed during the baking process. Discard the bay leaves. Transfer to a serving bowl. Sprinkle with the chopped parsley and lemon zest. Serve immediately with hot cooked noodles or rice.

Chicken with Almonds

SERVES 4

1/4 cup (1/2 stick) butter
4 boneless skinless chicken breast halves
2 tablespoons chopped onion
1 large garlic clove, minced
2 tablespoons flour
1 tablespoon tomato paste
1 1/2 cups chicken stock
2 tablespoons sherry
1/4 cup slivered almonds
1 teaspoon dried tarragon
Salt and freshly ground pepper to taste
3/4 cup sour cream
1/4 cup grated Parmesan cheese

Heat the butter in a skillet until melted. Add the chicken. Cook until brown on all sides. Remove the chicken with a slotted spoon to a platter, reserving the pan drippings. Cover the chicken to keep warm.

Stir the onion and garlic into the reserved pan drippings. Cook over low heat for 3 minutes, stirring frequently. Whisk in the flour and tomato paste until mixed. Stir in the stock and sherry. Bring to a boil, stirring occasionally. Add the chicken, almonds, tarragon, salt and pepper. Simmer, covered, for 45 to 50 minutes or until the chicken is cooked through, stirring occasionally.

Preheat the broiler. Transfer the chicken with a slotted spoon to a baking dish. Stir the sour cream into the remaining sauce. Cook just until heated through, stirring constantly. Spoon over the chicken. Sprinkle with the cheese. Broil until light brown. Serve with hot cooked white rice.

Coronado Chicken

SERVES 6

Peach Avocado Salsa
1 peach, peeled, chopped
1 small avocado, peeled, chopped
1 tomato, peeled, seeded, chopped
$1/4$ cup chopped jicama
3 tablespoons chopped red onion
2 tablespoons chopped fresh cilantro
3 tablespoons fresh lime juice
2 teaspoons olive oil
$1/4$ teaspoon red pepper flakes
Salt to taste
Chicken
6 boneless skinless chicken breast halves
4 teaspoons garlic-pepper seasoning
Juice of 1 orange
Juice of 1 lime
2 tablespoons olive oil
1 teaspoon dried oregano

For the salsa, combine the peach, avocado, tomato, jicama, onion and cilantro in a bowl and toss gently. Stir in a mixture of the lime juice, olive oil and red pepper flakes. Season with salt.

For the chicken, rub the chicken with the garlic-pepper seasoning. Arrange in a single layer in a shallow glass dish. Drizzle with the orange juice, lime juice and olive oil. Crush the oregano and sprinkle over the chicken. Chill, covered, for 30 minutes, turning once.

Drain the chicken, discarding the marinade. Transfer the chicken to a nonstick skillet. Cook over medium heat for 12 minutes or until the chicken is cooked through and light brown on both sides. Transfer to a serving platter. Serve topped with the salsa. Garnish with lime slices.

Currant Chicken

SERVES 12

Chicken
1 (8-ounce) jar Dijon mustard
$1/2$ cup plain yogurt
16 boneless skinless chicken breast halves
Seasoned bread crumbs
$1/3$ cup butter
Currant Sauce
1 cup red currant jelly
1 (6-ounce) can frozen orange juice concentrate
1 teaspoon dry mustard
$1/4$ teaspoon Tabasco sauce
$1/8$ teaspoon ginger powder

For the chicken, preheat the oven to 325 degrees. Combine the Dijon mustard and yogurt in a bowl and mix well. Brush both sides of the chicken with the mustard mixture. Coat with bread crumbs. Arrange in a single layer on a baking sheet sprayed with nonstick cooking spray. Top each half with 1 teaspoon of the butter.

Bake for 40 minutes or until the chicken is cooked through. May freeze the chicken before baking for up to 1 week. Thaw in the refrigerator 8 hours before baking.

For the sauce, combine the jelly, orange juice concentrate, dry mustard, Tabasco sauce and ginger powder in a saucepan and mix well. Bring to a boil, stirring occasionally; reduce heat. Simmer until time to serve. Drizzle over the chicken or serve on the side.

Lemon Chicken

SERVES 4

1/4 cup flour
1 garlic clove, minced
1/2 teaspoon salt
1/8 teaspoon freshly ground pepper
4 boneless skinless chicken breast halves
2 tablespoons olive oil
2 tablespoons butter
2 tablespoons fresh lemon juice
1/4 cup dry white wine or vermouth
2 small lemons, thinly sliced
1/4 cup chopped fresh parsley

Mix the flour, garlic, salt and pepper in a bowl. Pound the chicken 1/4 inch thick between sheets of waxed paper with a meat mallet or other heavy flat object. Coat the chicken with the flour mixture.

Heat the olive oil and butter in a skillet over medium heat until the butter melts. Add the chicken. Cook until light brown on both sides. Remove the chicken with a slotted spoon to a platter, reserving the pan drippings. Cover the chicken to keep warm.

Add the lemon juice and white wine to the reserved pan drippings and stir to deglaze the skillet. Return the chicken to the skillet. Add the lemon slices. Simmer, covered, over low heat for 30 minutes or until the chicken is cooked through. Remove the chicken with a slotted spoon to a serving platter. Drizzle with the sauce. Sprinkle with the parsley. Serve with basmati rice.

*A*t Persian and Greek banquets, the custom was to fill this drinking vessel with wine through the open top, but to drink from the stream of liquid that flowed directly into the mouth from the small spout in the front of the vessel.

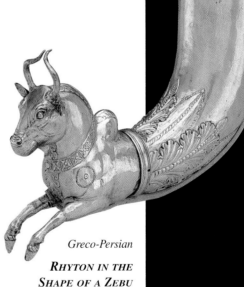

Greco-Persian

**RHYTON IN THE
SHAPE OF A ZEBU**
Silver, 200–100 B.C.

*Purchased with funds from the
Libbey Endowment, Gift of
Edward Drummond Libbey*

Moroccan Chicken

SERVES 3 OR 4

1 or 2 lemons, sliced
1 (3-pound) chicken, cut up
1/4 cup lemon juice
3 tablespoons olive oil
15 kalamata olives, sliced
1/4 to 1/2 cup golden raisins, or to taste
Salt and freshly ground pepper to taste

Preheat the oven to 400 degrees. Spread half the lemon slices in a 9×13-inch baking dish. Rub the chicken with the lemon juice and olive oil. Arrange the chicken over the lemon slices. Arrange the remaining lemon slices, olives and raisins around the chicken. Sprinkle with salt and pepper. Bake for 35 to 45 minutes or until the chicken is cooked through and brown.

Poulet Dijon

SERVES 6 TO 8

3 to 4 cups fresh English muffin crumbs
1 1/4 cups grated Parmesan cheese
1/3 cup chopped fresh parsley
1 1/2 cups (3 sticks) butter
2 1/2 tablespoons Dijon mustard
1 1/2 teaspoons Worcestershire sauce
3 garlic cloves, chopped
10 boneless skinless chicken breast halves

Mix the crumbs, cheese and parsley in a sealable plastic bag. Heat the butter, mustard, Worcestershire sauce and garlic in a saucepan until the butter melts; remove from heat. Dip the chicken in the butter mixture and coat with the crumb mixture. Place in a greased baking dish. Top with some of the butter and crumbs. Bake for 15 minutes at 350 degrees; turn chicken. Top with remaining butter and crumbs. Bake for 15 to 25 minutes longer or until cooked through.

Tarragon Chicken in Phyllo

SERVES 8

1 cup dry plain bread crumbs
1/2 cup grated Parmesan or Romano cheese
1 teaspoon dried tarragon, or 1 tablespoon fresh tarragon
1 teaspoon parsley flakes, or 1 tablespoon minced fresh parsley
1/2 teaspoon each salt and dry mustard
1/2 cup (1 stick) butter
8 boneless skinless chicken breast halves
Juice of 1 lemon
8 thick slices Muenster, mozzarella or Kasseri cheese
1/2 cup (1 stick) butter
8 sheets phyllo pastry

Combine the bread crumbs, Parmesan cheese, tarragon, parsley flakes, salt and dry mustard in a bowl and mix well. Spread on a sheet of waxed paper. Melt 1/2 cup butter in a saucepan. Dip each chicken breast in the butter and coat with the bread crumb mixture. Arrange on a sheet of waxed paper to dry. Drizzle with the lemon juice. Top each chicken breast with a slice of the Muenster cheese. Melt 1/2 cup butter in a saucepan.

Preheat the oven to 325 degrees. Cover the phyllo with waxed paper topped with a damp towel to prevent it from drying out, removing 1 sheet at a time. Arrange 1 sheet of the pastry on a flat surface. Brush liberally with some of the butter. Place 1 chicken breast at the bottom of the short end of the pastry and fold over to enclose the chicken. Fold the long sides over the chicken and continue rolling to the end of the pastry. Arrange seam side down on a lightly greased baking sheet. Repeat the process with the remaining butter, remaining phyllo and remaining chicken.

Brush the tops of the pastry with the remaining melted butter. Bake for 1 hour or until the chicken is cooked through and the pastry is golden brown. Serve with fresh steamed asparagus and fettuccini Alfredo. May prepare in advance and store, covered, in the refrigerator, bringing to room temperature 30 minutes before baking.

Barbecued Turkey

SERVES 10

1/2 cup water
1/4 cup vinegar
1/4 cup packed brown sugar
1 tablespoon lemon juice
1 tablespoon butter
2 teaspoons prepared mustard
1 teaspoon salt
1/4 teaspoon black pepper
1/4 teaspoon ketchup
1/8 teaspoon cayenne pepper
2 tablespoons Worcestershire sauce
1 teaspoon smoked salt
1 (10-pound) turkey

Preheat the grill. Combine the water, vinegar, brown sugar, lemon juice, butter, prepared mustard, salt, black pepper, ketchup and cayenne pepper in a saucepan and mix well. Simmer for 20 minutes, stirring occasionally. Stir in the Worcestershire sauce and smoked salt. Bring to a boil, stirring occasionally. Remove from heat. Cover to keep warm.

Place the turkey on the grill rack and close the lid. Grill over hot coals for 11 minutes per pound or until the turkey is cooked through, basting frequently with the sauce during the last 30 minutes of the grilling process. Remove from grill and wrap in foil. Let stand for up to 30 minutes.

Note: The sauce may be doubled for a larger turkey. Allow 1 pound of turkey per person.

Gala Turkey

SERVES 8

1 (6-pound) turkey breast with bone
1 1/2 cups fresh lemon or lime juice
1 cup chopped fresh parsley
1 cup olive oil
6 garlic cloves, minced
5 teaspoons dried rosemary
1 teaspoon salt
1/2 to 3/4 cup mayonnaise
1/2 to 3/4 cup sour cream
1 jar capers, drained

Place the turkey in a large cooking bag. Combine the lemon juice, parsley, olive oil, garlic, rosemary and salt in a bowl and mix well. Pour over the turkey; seal tightly. Marinate in the refrigerator for 4 to 10 hours, turning occasionally. Bring the turkey to room temperature before baking. Drain, reserving the marinade.

Preheat the oven to 400 degrees. Pat the turkey dry with paper towels. Place on a rack on a roasting pan. Roast for 1 to 1 1/2 hours or until a meat thermometer registers 165 degrees, basting with the reserved marinade occasionally. Transfer to a serving platter.

Bring the remaining marinade to a boil in a saucepan. Combine the mayonnaise, sour cream and capers in a bowl and mix well. Add 1/4 to 1/2 cup of the marinade, stirring until the sauce is of a medium-thick consistency. Serve with hot or cold turkey.

Note: Grill the turkey over hot coals if preferred.

Roasted Cornish Hens with Honey Mustard Glaze

SERVES 4

Honey Mustard Glaze
$1/2$ cup honey
$1/2$ cup spicy brown mustard
3 tablespoons balsamic vinegar
2 tablespoons chopped fresh cilantro
1 tablespoon crushed juniper berries
1 teaspoon cumin

Cornish Game Hens
4 (1-pound) Cornish game hens
Salt and freshly ground pepper to taste
4 bay leaves
2 tablespoons dried thyme
$1/2$ teaspoon crushed chile peppers
4 garlic cloves, crushed
2 tablespoons olive oil

For the glaze, combine the honey, brown mustard, balsamic vinegar, cilantro, juniper berries and cumin in a bowl and mix well.

For the game hens, preheat the oven to 375 degrees. Sprinkle the inside and outside of the game hens with salt and pepper. Place equal portions of the bay leaves, thyme, chile peppers and garlic in the inside cavity of each game hen. Brush with the olive oil.

Arrange the game hens breast side down in a roasting pan. Roast for 20 minutes; turn. Roast for 20 minutes. Brush with the glaze. Roast for 10 minutes longer to allow the glaze to brown. Serve immediately with wild rice salad.

Roast Duck with Peaches, Almonds and Ginger

SERVES 4

Duck
2 (5-pound) ducks
3 tablespoons fresh lemon juice
3 tablespoons fresh orange juice
2 tablespoons grated gingerroot
1 tablespoon curry powder
1 tablespoon grated lemon zest
1 tablespoon grated orange zest

Peach Sauce
$1/2$ cup duck or chicken stock
$1/4$ cup fresh orange juice
$1/4$ cup almonds, toasted, finely ground
2 tablespoons brown sugar
2 tablespoons fresh lemon juice
1 tablespoon grated gingerroot
2 freestone peaches, peeled, cut into quarters

For the duck, preheat the oven to 500 degrees. Discard the necks, wing tips and excess fat from the ducks. Prick the outer surface with a fork. Combine the lemon juice, orange juice, gingerroot, curry powder and lemon and orange zest in a bowl and mix well. Rub the ducks inside and out with the lemon juice mixture. Place on a rack in a roasting pan. Roast for 1 hour or until the ducks test done. Remove from oven. Decrease the oven temperature to 450 degrees. Cool the ducks slightly. Cut into quarters or eighths. Arrange in a baking dish.

For the sauce, combine the stock, orange juice, almonds, brown sugar, lemon juice and gingerroot in a saucepan and mix well. Bring to a simmer, stirring occasionally. Stir in the peaches. Simmer for 5 minutes or just until heated through, stirring occasionally.

To serve, heat the duck in the oven for 5 minutes or just until hot. Transfer the duck to a serving platter. Drizzle with the warm sauce. Serve with wild rice pilaf and sautéed spinach.

Roasted Pheasant with Port and Pear Salsa

SERVES 4

Port and Pear Salsa

1 large pink grapefruit
2 medium pears
$^1/_2$ cup dried cranberries
2 tablespoons finely chopped red onion
2 tablespoons fresh lime juice
$^1/_2$ teaspoon finely chopped garlic
$^1/_2$ teaspoon finely chopped jalapeño chile
$^1/_2$ teaspoon grated lime zest

Pheasant

2 (2$^1/_2$-pound) pheasants
Juice of 2 oranges
$^1/_4$ cup olive oil
Salt and pepper to taste
8 sprigs of Italian parsley
4 garlic cloves, crushed
2 bay leaves
12 slices bacon
$^1/_2$ cup chicken broth
$^1/_4$ cup tawny port

For the salsa, peel the grapefruit and remove the white pith. Separate into sections. Cut each section crosswise over a bowl into thirds. Peel the pears and cut into $^1/_4$-inch pieces. Add to the grapefruit immediately to prevent the pears from turning brown. Add the cranberries, onion, lime juice, garlic, chile and lime zest and mix gently. May prepare in advance and store, covered, in the refrigerator.

For the pheasant, preheat the oven to 350 degrees. Rinse the pheasants and discard any excess fat; pat dry. Arrange in a shallow roasting pan. Drizzle inside and out with the orange juice. Brush with the olive oil and sprinkle with salt and pepper inside and out. Place 4 sprigs of parsley, 2 garlic cloves and 1 bay leaf in each pheasant cavity. Arrange 6 slices of bacon over the top of each pheasant. Add the broth and port to the roasting pan.

Roast for 1 hour, basting several times with the pan juices. Discard the bacon. Roast for 30 minutes longer or until brown and cooked through, basting with the pan juices. The juices should run clear when the thickest part of the thigh is pierced with the tip of a knife. Remove the pheasant to a serving platter. Let rest for 10 minutes before carving. Garnish with kumquats. Serve with the salsa.

The recipe featured here is Chocolate Pears.

Chocolate Bonbon Cake

SERVES 12

Cake
1 cup (2 sticks) butter, softened
1 cup sugar
4 egg yolks
2 cups sifted flour
4 egg whites
1 cup sour cream
3/4 cup slivered almonds, finely chopped
1/2 cup orange marmalade
6 tablespoons currant jelly
Chocolate Bonbon Frosting
1 cup semisweet chocolate chips
1/4 cup (1/2 stick) butter
2 cups sifted confectioners' sugar
3 tablespoons hot water

For the cake, beat the butter in a mixing bowl until light and fluffy, scraping the bowl occasionally. Add the sugar gradually, beating until creamy after each addition. Add the egg yolks and beat until smooth. Stir in the flour until blended. Beat the egg whites in a mixing bowl until soft peaks form. Fold into the batter.

Preheat the oven to 350 degrees. Invert 2 round 9-inch cake pans. Coat the outside bottoms of the cake pans with butter and dust lightly with flour. Spread about 1/2 cup of the batter over the bottom of each pan almost to the edge with a spatula. Bake for 10 minutes or until golden brown around the edges. Remove the thin cakes carefully to a wire rack to cool. Cool the pans and wash. Repeat the process 3 more times with the remaining batter, buttering and dusting the bottoms of the cake pans with flour each time. Combine the sour cream and almonds in a bowl and mix well.

Place 1 cake layer top side up on a cake plate. Spread with 2 tablespoons of the orange marmalade and 3 tablespoons of the sour cream mixture. Arrange another cake layer over the sour cream mixture. Spread with 2 tablespoons of the currant jelly and 3 tablespoons of the sour cream mixture. Repeat the process with the remaining cake layers, alternating marmalade-sour cream layers with jelly-sour cream layers, leaving the top layer plain. Place a heavy glass pie plate on top of the cake to weigh down the layers. Chill, covered, for 8 to 10 hours. Trim the uneven edges.

For the frosting, heat the chocolate chips and butter in a double boiler over hot water until blended, stirring frequently. Remove from heat. Add the confectioners' sugar alternately with 3 tablespoons hot water, beating until of a spreading consistency. Spread over the top and side of the cake. Chill, covered, until serving time.

Note: Create a decorative garnish by arranging 3 blanched whole almonds around a candied cherry in a floral pattern. Scatter several arrangements on top of the cake.

Warm Chocolate Cakes

SERVES 8

8 ounces bittersweet chocolate
1 cup (2 sticks) butter
4 eggs
4 egg yolks
1/2 cup sugar
4 teaspoons flour
1 pint vanilla ice cream (optional)

Coat eight 4-ounce molds, custard cups or ramekins with butter and dust lightly with flour; tap to remove excess flour. Butter the molds, custard cups or ramekins again and dust lightly with flour. Preheat the oven to 450 degrees.

Heat the chocolate and 1 cup butter in a double boiler over simmering water until almost blended, stirring occasionally. Beat the eggs, egg yolks and sugar in a mixing bowl until thickened. Whisk the warm chocolate mixture until blended. Add the egg mixture gradually, beating constantly until blended. Add 4 teaspoons flour and stir just until combined. Pour the batter into the prepared molds. Arrange the molds on a baking sheet. May chill the molds at this point until just before baking, bringing the molds to room temperature before baking.

Bake for 10 minutes; the centers will still be soft but the edges of the cakes will be set. Invert each mold onto a dessert plate and let stand for about 10 seconds. Unmold by lifting 1 corner of each mold, allowing the cakes to fall onto the plates. Serve immediately with ice cream.

Souffléed Truffle Cake

SERVES 8 TO 10

Cake
1 pound semisweet chocolate
1/2 cup (1 stick) unsalted butter
2 tablespoons brandy
1 tablespoon flour
4 egg yolks, at room temperature, lightly beaten
4 egg whites
1/8 teaspoon salt
1/8 teaspoon cream of tartar
Crème Anglaise with Brandy
1 cup heavy cream
4 egg yolks
1/3 cup sugar
2 tablespoons brandy

For the cake, heat the chocolate and butter in a heavy saucepan over low heat until melted, stirring frequently. Combine the chocolate mixture with the brandy, flour and egg yolks in a bowl and mix well.

Preheat the oven to 425 degrees. Beat the egg whites, salt and cream of tartar in a mixing bowl until stiff but glossy peaks form. Fold into the chocolate mixture in 3 additions. Spoon the batter into a greased and floured 8-inch springform pan. Bake for 20 minutes; the center will appear uncooked. Chill, covered, in the refrigerator.

For the sauce, whisk the heavy cream, egg yolks and sugar in a small heavy saucepan until blended. Cook over medium-low heat until thickened enough to coat the back of a spoon, stirring constantly with a wooden spoon; do not allow to boil. Strain into a bowl and stir in the brandy. May prepare the sauce in advance and store, covered, in the refrigerator. Reheat before serving.

To serve, puddle some of the warm Crème Anglaise on dessert plates. Cut the cake into wedges and arrange over the sauce. Garnish lightly with confectioners' sugar.

Frozen Lemon Cake

SERVES 12

2 (3-ounce) packages ladyfingers
2 (14-ounce) cans sweetened condensed milk
8 egg yolks
3/4 cup plus 2 to 3 tablespoons fresh lemon juice
2 teaspoons grated lemon zest
8 egg whites
1/4 teaspoon cream of tartar
Confectioners' sugar
1 thin lemon slice, twisted (optional)

Preheat the oven to 375 degrees. Line the bottom of a greased 9-inch springform pan with some of the ladyfingers, trimming the ladyfingers to fit if needed. Stand the remaining ladyfingers around the edge of the pan, cutting the bottom ends so the tops of the ladyfingers are even with the top edge of the pan.

Whisk the condensed milk, egg yolks, lemon juice and lemon zest in a bowl. Beat the egg whites and cream of tartar in a mixing bowl until stiff peaks form. Fold into the lemon mixture. Spoon into the prepared pan. Bake for 20 to 25 minutes or until light brown. Cool in pan on a wire rack. Freeze, covered with foil, for up to 3 months.

To serve, remove the side of the pan and place the cake on a cake plate. Dust lightly with confectioners' sugar and arrange the lemon slice in the center of the cake. Let stand at room temperature for 15 minutes before serving. Leftovers may be refrozen.

White Chocolate Raspberry Cheesecake

SERVES 12

Almond Crust
2 cups graham cracker crumbs
1 cup slivered almonds, finely ground
1/2 cup (1 stick) butter, melted
White Chocolate Filling
32 ounces cream cheese, softened
6 ounces sugar
2 egg yolks
4 eggs
2 tablespoons flour
1 teaspoon vanilla extract
8 ounces white chocolate, melted
2 pints fresh red raspberries

For the crust, preheat the oven to 350 degrees. Combine the graham cracker crumbs, almonds and butter in a medium bowl and mix well. Pat the crumb mixture over the bottom and up the side of a 10-inch springform pan. Bake for 10 minutes or until golden brown. Maintain oven temperature.

For the filling, beat the cream cheese in a mixing bowl at low speed until fluffy, scraping the bowl occasionally. Add the sugar and beat until blended. Beat in the egg yolks. Add the eggs, flour and vanilla and beat until smooth. Add the white chocolate gradually, beating constantly until blended. Fold in the raspberries.

Spoon the cream cheese mixture into the prepared pan. Bake for 75 minutes. Cool slightly. Chill, covered, for 8 to 10 hours. Cut into wedges. Garnish each serving with shaved white chocolate and additional fresh raspberries.

Key Lime Cheesecake

Gingersnap Crust
1¹/4 cups gingersnap cookie crumbs
2 tablespoons sugar
5 tablespoons unsalted butter, melted

Key Lime Filling
24 ounces cream cheese, softened
1¹/2 cups sugar
4 large eggs
¹/4 cup Key lime juice
2 tablespoons grated lime zest

Sour Cream Topping
2 cups sour cream
¹/3 cup sugar
2 tablespoons Key lime juice
2 tablespoons grated lime zest

For the crust, preheat the oven to 350 degrees. Combine the cookie crumbs and sugar in a bowl and mix with a fork. Stir in the butter. Press the crumb mixture over the bottom and half way up the side of a 9-inch springform pan.

For the filling, beat the cream cheese and sugar in a mixing bowl at low speed until smooth, scraping the bowl occasionally. Add the eggs 1 at a time, beating well after each addition. Add the Key lime juice and lime zest and mix well. Spoon the cream cheese mixture into the prepared pan. Bake for 40 minutes or until the edge pulls from the side of the pan and is light brown; the center will not be completely set.

For the topping, whisk the sour cream, sugar, Key lime juice and lime zest in a bowl. Spread over the top of the cheesecake. Bake for 10 minutes longer. Cool in pan on a wire rack. Chill, covered, for 4 to 10 hours. Garnish with lime slices, lime zest and/or fresh strawberries, raspberries or blueberries.

Pumpkin Cheesecake

Butter Crust
¹/3 cup sugar
¹/3 cup butter, softened
1 egg
1¹/4 cups flour

Pumpkin Filling
16 ounces cream cheese, softened
³/4 cup sugar
1 (16-ounce) can pumpkin
1 teaspoon cinnamon
1 teaspoon nutmeg
¹/2 teaspoon allspice
¹/2 teaspoon cloves
¹/4 teaspoon ground ginger
¹/8 teaspoon salt
2 eggs

For the crust, preheat the oven to 400 degrees. Beat the sugar and butter in a mixing bowl until light and fluffy. Add the egg and beat until blended. Beat in the flour until smooth. Press over the bottom and 2 inches up the side of a 9-inch springform pan. Bake for 5 minutes. Reduce the oven temperature to 350 degrees.

For the filling, beat the cream cheese and sugar in a mixing bowl at medium speed until light and fluffy, scraping the bowl occasionally. Add the pumpkin, cinnamon, nutmeg, allspice, cloves, ginger and salt and mix well. Add the eggs 1 at a time, beating well after each addition. Spoon the cream cheese mixture into the prepared pan. Bake for 50 minutes. Cool in pan on a wire rack. Chill, covered, until serving time.

Note: May prepare up to 1 day in advance.

Creamy Caramels

MAKES 64

1 tablespoon canola oil or flavorless oil
1¹/2 cups heavy cream
1 cup light corn syrup
³/4 cup sugar
3 tablespoons unsalted butter, softened
2 teaspoons vanilla extract

Line an 8×8-inch metal baking pan with foil, allowing a 1-inch overhang. Coat the foil with the canola oil.

Combine the heavy cream, corn syrup, sugar and butter in a heavy 3-quart saucepan. Cook over medium heat for 5 minutes or until the sugar dissolves, stirring constantly with a wooden spoon. Dip a pastry brush in warm water and brush down the side of the pan twice during the cooking process. Increase the heat to medium-high and place a candy thermometer in the pan.

Cook for 30 minutes or until the thermometer registers 250 degrees, stirring constantly. Remove from heat. Stir in the vanilla. Pour into the prepared pan. Let stand until firm. Cut into squares. Wrap each square in waxed paper, twisting the ends to seal.

Haystacks

MAKES 50 TO 60

1 pound white chocolate
1¹/2 cups salted Spanish peanuts
1¹/2 cups salted thin pretzel sticks, broken into thirds

Line a baking sheet with waxed paper. Heat the white chocolate in a double boiler over simmering water until melted, stirring frequently. Remove from heat. Stir in the peanuts and pretzels. Drop the chocolate mixture by teaspoonfuls onto the waxed paper. Chill until firm. Store the candy in tins or sealable plastic bags.

Meringue-Coated Pecans

SERVES 8 TO 10

1 cup sugar
1 teaspoon cinnamon
1 teaspoon nutmeg
¹/2 teaspoon salt
¹/4 teaspoon ground cloves
2 egg whites
2 tablespoons water
2 cups pecan halves

Preheat the oven to 300 degrees. Combine the sugar, cinnamon, nutmeg, salt and cloves in a bowl and mix well. Beat the egg whites and water in a mixing bowl until fluffy. Pour over the pecans in a bowl and stir to coat. Add the sugar mixture and mix well. Spread the pecan mixture on a buttered baking sheet with sides. Bake for 25 minutes, stirring several times during the baking process. Let stand until cool. Break into bite-size pieces. Store in an airtight container in the refrigerator or freezer.

Chocolate and Hazelnut Biscotti

MAKES 4 DOZEN

1 cup sugar
1/2 cup (1 stick) unsalted butter, softened
2 extra-large eggs, at room temperature
2 cups unbleached flour
1 1/2 cups hazelnuts, chopped
5 tablespoons Dutch processed baking cocoa
2 3/4 teaspoons vanilla extract
2 1/2 teaspoons almond extract
1 1/2 teaspoons baking powder
Salt to taste
Cinnamon to taste

Preheat the oven to 325 degrees. Beat the sugar and butter in a mixing bowl for 2 to 3 minutes or until light and fluffy, scraping the bowl occasionally. Add the eggs 1 at a time, beating well after each addition. Add the flour and mix well. Beat in the hazelnuts, baking cocoa, flavorings, baking powder, salt and cinnamon.

Shape the dough into 3 logs 1 to 2 inches in diameter on an ungreased aluminum baking sheet. Bake on the center oven rack for 35 to 40 minutes or until the logs are puffy and have small cracks on the surface. Cool for several minutes.

Reduce the oven temperature to 275 degrees. Cut the logs into 1/2-inch slices. Arrange the slices cut side down on the baking sheet. Bake for 20 to 30 minutes or until dry and crisp. Remove to a wire rack to cool. Store in an airtight container.

Chocolate Dip Cookies

MAKES 3 DOZEN

1 cup (2 sticks) butter, softened
1 cup sifted confectioners' sugar
1 teaspoon vanilla extract
1/8 teaspoon salt
2 cups flour
1 cup semisweet chocolate chips
1/2 cup finely chopped walnuts
3/4 cup semisweet chocolate chips
1/4 cup (1/2 stick) butter
1 1/2 tablespoons cream
1/8 teaspoon salt

Preheat the oven to 350 degrees. Beat 1 cup butter and confectioners' sugar in a mixing bowl until light and fluffy, scraping the bowl occasionally. Beat in the vanilla and 1/8 teaspoon salt. Add the flour and beat until blended. Stir in 1 cup chocolate chips and walnuts. Shape the dough into 3/4-inch balls and arrange on a lightly greased cookie sheet. Flatten with a glass. Bake for 15 minutes. Cool on cookie sheet for 2 minutes. Remove to a wire rack to cool completely.

Combine 3/4 cup chocolate chips, 1/4 cup butter, cream and 1/8 teaspoon salt in a double boiler over hot water. Cook until blended, stirring frequently. Dip half of each cookie in the chocolate. Arrange the cookies on a cookie sheet lined with waxed paper. Chill until set. May freeze for future use.

andies and crystallized fruits were displayed on this delicately modelled shell dish. The beauty of the porcelain is enhanced by naturalistic details, sinuous curving lines, and touches of gold.

Meissen Manufactory
Germany

NEREID SWEETMEAT STAND
Porcelain with enamel colors and gilding, 1737

Purchased with funds from the Florence Scott Libbey Bequest, in Memory of her Father, Maurice A. Scott

Chocolate Truffle Cookies

MAKES 6¹/₂ DOZEN

2¹/₄ cups flour
¹/₄ teaspoon nutmeg
¹/₄ teaspoon salt
¹/₄ cup (¹/₂ stick) butter, softened
¹/₄ cup heavy cream
2 tablespoons honey
1 cup semisweet chocolate chips
2 tablespoons bourbon
1 teaspoon vanilla extract
³/₄ cup (1¹/₂ sticks) butter, softened
¹/₂ cup confectioners' sugar
1¹/₂ cups chopped pecans, toasted, coarsely ground

Mix the flour, nutmeg and salt together. Combine ¹/₄ cup butter, heavy cream and honey in a saucepan. Cook over medium-low heat until blended, stirring frequently. Remove from heat. Add the chocolate chips and stir until smooth. Stir in the bourbon and vanilla gently.

Beat ³/₄ cup butter and confectioners' sugar in a mixing bowl until creamy, scraping the bowl occasionally. Add the chocolate mixture and flour mixture and mix until a soft dough forms. Chill, covered, for 1 hour.

Preheat the oven to 375 degrees. Shape the dough into 1-inch balls. Roll in the pecans. Arrange 2 inches apart on an ungreased cookie sheet. Bake for 8 minutes or until firm. Cool on cookie sheet for 2 minutes. Remove to a wire rack to cool completely. Store in an airtight container.

Note: The use of a cookie scoop makes this type of cookie much easier to prepare.

Fudgy Bonbons

MAKES 5 DOZEN

2 cups semisweet chocolate chips
$1/4$ cup ($1/2$ stick) butter
1 (14-ounce) can sweetened condensed milk
2 cups flour
1 teaspoon vanilla extract
60 milk chocolate candy kisses
2 ounces white baking chocolate or vanilla chips
1 teaspoon vegetable oil or shortening

Combine the chocolate chips and butter in a saucepan. Cook over low heat until smooth, stirring frequently. Stir in the condensed milk.

Combine the chocolate mixture, flour and vanilla in a bowl and mix well. Shape 1 tablespoon of the dough around each candy kiss, covering completely. Arrange 1 inch apart on an ungreased cookie sheet. Chill in the refrigerator.

Preheat the oven to 350 degrees. Bake for 6 to 8 minutes; cookies will be soft and shiny but will become firm as they cool. Cool on cookie sheet for 2 minutes. Remove to a wire rack to cool completely. Combine the white chocolate and oil in a saucepan. Cook over low heat until smooth, stirring constantly. Drizzle over the cookies. Let stand until set. Store in an airtight container.

Turtle Bars

MAKES 3 DOZEN

Crust
2 cups flour
1 cup butter, cut into chunks, chilled
3 tablespoons sugar
1 teaspoon salt
Filling
$1/2$ cup (1 stick) plus 2 tablespoons butter
1 cup packed brown sugar
$1/3$ cup honey
$1/4$ cup sugar
3 tablespoons whipping cream
1 tablespoon vanilla extract
4 cups pecan halves
Chocolate Glaze
8 ounces semisweet chocolate
1 cup whipping cream
1 teaspoon vanilla extract

For the crust, combine the flour, butter, sugar and salt in a mixing bowl. Beat at medium speed just until the mixture adheres. Press over the bottom and up the sides of an ungreased 9×13-inch baking pan. Chill in the refrigerator.

For the filling, preheat the oven to 350 degrees. Combine the butter, brown sugar, honey and sugar in a saucepan. Cook over medium heat until smooth and just barely boiling, stirring frequently. Remove from heat. Stir in the whipping cream and vanilla. Sprinkle the pecans over the chilled layer. Pour the filling over the pecans. Bake for 25 to 30 minutes or until light brown and bubbly. Let stand until cool.

For the glaze, combine the chocolate, whipping cream and vanilla in a saucepan. Cook until smooth, stirring frequently. Drizzle over the prepared layers. Chill, covered, in the refrigerator. Cut into bars.

Devil's Food Cookies

MAKES 4½ DOZEN COOKIES

2 cups sifted flour
½ teaspoon baking soda
¼ teaspoon salt
1 cup packed brown sugar
½ cup (1 stick) butter, softened
1 egg
1 teaspoon vanilla extract
2 ounces unsweetened chocolate, melted, cooled
¾ cup sour cream
½ cup chopped walnuts

Preheat the oven to 350 degrees. Sift the flour, baking soda and salt together. Beat the brown sugar and butter in a mixing bowl until light and fluffy. Add the egg and vanilla and beat until blended. Stir in the chocolate. Add the dry ingredients alternately with the sour cream, mixing well after each addition. Stir in the walnuts. Drop by teaspoonfuls 2 inches apart onto a greased cookie sheet. Bake for 10 minutes or until light brown. Cool on cookie sheet for 2 minutes. Remove to a wire rack to cool completely.

Javanese Cookies

MAKES 3 DOZEN

1 cup (2 sticks) butter, softened
¾ cup sugar
2 cups flour
1 cup shredded coconut

Beat the butter and sugar in a mixing bowl until creamy, scraping the bowl occasionally. Add the flour and beat until blended. Stir in the coconut. Shape the dough into a log 3 inches in diameter. Chill, wrapped in waxed paper, for several hours.

Preheat the oven to 300 degrees. Cut the log into ¼-inch slices. Arrange the slices on a cookie sheet. Bake for 20 minutes or until light brown. Garnish the warm cookies with confectioners' sugar. Cool on cookie sheet for 2 minutes. Remove to a wire rack to cool completely.

Gram's Best Cookies

MAKES 4 DOZEN

1 cup (2 sticks) butter, softened
1 cup sugar
1 cup packed brown sugar
1 egg
1 cup vegetable oil
1 teaspoon vanilla extract
1 cup rolled oats
1 cup crushed cornflakes
½ cup shredded coconut
½ cup chopped pecans
3½ cups sifted flour
½ teaspoon baking soda
½ teaspoon salt

Preheat the oven to 325 degrees. Beat the butter, sugar and brown sugar in a mixing bowl until light and fluffy, scraping the bowl occasionally. Add the egg and mix until blended. Beat in the oil and vanilla. Stir in the oats, cornflakes, coconut and pecans. Add a mixture of the flour, baking soda and salt and mix well.

Shape the dough into 1-inch balls. Arrange on an ungreased cookie sheet. Flatten with a fork dipped in water. Bake for 12 minutes. Cool on cookie sheet for 2 minutes. Remove to a wire rack to cool completely.

Lemon Drop Cookies

MAKES 3 DOZEN

2 cups flour
1 cup (2 sticks) butter, softened
1/2 cup confectioners' sugar
3/4 cup sugar
1 egg, beaten
3 tablespoons lemon juice
Grated zest of 1 lemon
1 1/2 tablespoons butter
Confectioners' sugar to taste

Preheat the oven to 350 degrees. Combine the flour, 1 cup butter and 1/2 cup confectioners' sugar in a mixing bowl. Beat until smooth. Shape the dough into 1-inch balls. Arrange on a greased cookie sheet.

Make an indentation in each cookie with the back of a spoon or your thumb. Bake for 10 to 12 minutes or until light brown. Cool on cookie sheet for 2 minutes. Remove to a wire rack to cool completely.

Combine the sugar, egg, lemon juice, lemon zest and 1 1/2 tablespoons butter in a saucepan. Cook over medium heat until thickened, stirring constantly. Let stand until cool. Spoon some of the lemon sauce into each cookie indentation. Sift confectioners' sugar to taste over the tops of the cookies.

Framboise Cream Cheese Bars

MAKES 14

1/2 cup packed brown sugar
1/4 cup (1/2 stick) butter, softened
1 cup flour
1/2 cup chopped pecans
1/4 cup red raspberry preserves
8 ounces cream cheese, softened
1/4 cup sugar
2 tablespoons lemon juice
2 tablespoons milk
1 egg
1/2 teaspoon vanilla extract

Preheat the oven to 350 degrees. Beat the brown sugar and butter in a mixing bowl until creamy. Stir in the flour and pecans. Pat 1 cup of the pecan mixture into a greased 8×8-inch baking pan. Bake for 15 minutes. Let stand until cool. Spread with the preserves. Maintain the oven temperature.

Beat the cream cheese, sugar, lemon juice, milk, egg and vanilla in a mixing bowl for 4 minutes, scraping the bowl occasionally. Spoon over the prepared layers. Sprinkle with the remaining pecan mixture. Bake for 30 minutes. Cool in pan on a wire rack. Cut into 1-inch bars.

San Franciscan Apple Pie

SERVES 8 TO 10

Filling

$1/2$ cup (1 stick) unsalted butter

10 medium tart apples, peeled, sliced

$1/4$ cup sugar

$1/2$ cup apricot preserves

2 tablespoons finely grated lemon zest

$1/4$ cup dark rum

1 cup sour cream

$1/4$ cup packed brown sugar

2 eggs

1 tablespoon flour

$2^1/2$ teaspoons vanilla extract

1 teaspoon cinnamon

$1/4$ teaspoon salt

Pie Shell

1 (11-ounce) jar apricot preserves

$1/4$ cup apricot brandy or orange liqueur

1 baked (10-inch) deep-dish pie shell

Assembly

$1/2$ cup shredded coconut

$1/2$ cup coarsely chopped walnuts or pecans

For the filling, heat the butter in a large skillet until melted. Stir in the apples and sugar. Cook, covered, over medium-low heat for 10 minutes, stirring occasionally; remove cover. Cook until the apples are tender but firm, stirring occasionally. Stir in the apricot preserves and lemon zest. Cook over medium heat for 2 minutes, stirring frequently. Heat the rum in a saucepan. Ignite and pour over the apple mixture.

Preheat the oven to 375 degrees. Combine the sour cream, brown sugar, eggs, flour, vanilla, cinnamon and salt in a mixing bowl. Beat until blended, scraping the bowl occasionally. Stir half the sour cream mixture into the apple mixture. Taste for flavor, adding additional sugar and lemon zest if needed.

For the pie shell, combine the preserves and brandy in a food processor container. Process until puréed. Brush the side and bottom of the pie shell with 2 teaspoons of the preserve mixture, storing the remaining glaze in the refrigerator.

To assemble, spoon the apple mixture into the prepared pie shell. Spread with the remaining sour cream mixture. Sprinkle with the coconut and walnuts. Bake in the upper third of the oven until the coconut and walnuts are light brown. Serve warm.

Apple Cranberry Crumb Pie

SERVES 8

Filling

5 to 6 large apples, peeled, sliced

1 cup fresh cranberries

$1/2$ cup chopped pecans

$3/4$ cup sugar

2 tablespoons cornstarch

1 teaspoon cinnamon

1 unbaked (9-inch) pie shell

Crumb Topping

1 cup flour

$1/2$ cup packed brown sugar

$1/3$ cup rolled oats

$3/4$ teaspoon cinnamon

$1/2$ cup (1 stick) butter, chopped

For the filling, preheat the oven to 350 degrees. Combine the apples, cranberries and pecans in a bowl and toss gently. Stir in a mixture of the sugar, cornstarch and 1 teaspoon cinnamon. Spoon into the pie shell.

For the topping, combine the flour, brown sugar, oats and $3/4$ teaspoon cinnamon in a bowl and mix well. Cut in the butter until crumbly. Sprinkle over the apple mixture. Bake for 1 hour.

Four-Berry Pie

2 cups fresh or drained frozen blueberries
2 cups fresh or drained frozen strawberries, cut into halves
2 cups fresh or drained frozen raspberries
2 cups fresh or drained frozen blackberries
3 tablespoons fresh lemon juice
2 cups sugar
1 1/4 cups flour, or 1/2 cup quick-cooking tapioca
1/4 teaspoon freshly grated nutmeg
1/8 teaspoon salt
2 refrigerator pie pastries
1 tablespoon cinnamon-sugar
Vanilla ice cream

Toss the blueberries, strawberries, raspberries and blackberries gently in a bowl. Drizzle with the lemon juice. Combine the sugar, flour, nutmeg and salt in a bowl and mix well. Spread evenly over the fruit mixture and toss gently. If using tapioca, let the mixture stand for 15 minutes before proceeding.

Preheat the oven to 325 degrees. Line a 10-inch deep-dish pie plate with 1 of the pastries. Sprinkle the cinnamon-sugar over the top of the remaining pastry. Spoon the fruit mixture into the pastry-lined pie plate, mounding slightly in the center. Arrange the pastry cinnamon-sugar side down over the fruit mixture. Flute the edge and cut vents. Place on a foil-lined round baking pan on the center oven rack. Bake for 60 minutes. Increase the oven temperature to 350 degrees. Bake for 30 minutes longer. Let stand for 30 minutes before serving. Serve warm or at room temperature with vanilla ice cream.

Note: May prepare up to 1 day in advance of serving.

Lemon Ice Cream Pie

Walnut Crust
1 cup walnuts
1/4 cup (1/2 stick) unsalted butter, softened
1/4 cup sugar
1 tablespoon flour
Filling
1 1/2 cups sugar
1/2 cup (1 stick) butter
1/2 cup lemon juice
1 tablespoon grated lemon zest
3 eggs, beaten
3 egg yolks, beaten
1/2 gallon vanilla ice cream, softened

For the crust, preheat the oven to 450 degrees. Line a 10-inch springform pan with foil. Combine the walnuts, 1/4 cup butter, 1/4 cup sugar and flour in a food processor container. Process until finely chopped. Press the crumb mixture over the bottom of the prepared pan. Bake for 5 minutes or until light brown. Cool on a wire rack.

For the filling, combine 1 1/2 cups sugar, 1/2 cup butter, lemon juice, lemon zest, eggs and egg yolks in a double boiler over simmering water. Cook for 10 to 20 minutes or until thickened, stirring constantly. Spoon into a bowl. Let stand, loosely covered, until cool.

Spread half the ice cream in the prepared pan. Freeze for 30 minutes or until firm. Spread with half the lemon sauce. Freeze for 30 minutes. Spread with the remaining ice cream. Freeze for 30 minutes. Top with the remaining lemon sauce. Freeze for 8 to 10 hours, covering after 30 minutes. Remove the side of the pan. Discard the foil. Cut into wedges. Garnish with lemon twists and mint leaves.

Note: May prepare up to 3 days in advance.

Macadamia Banana Cream Pie

SERVES 8

Macadamia Crust
1/2 cup chopped macadamia nuts
1/2 cup flaked coconut
2 tablespoons light brown sugar
1 egg white
1 unbaked (10-inch) deep-dish pie shell

Custard Filling
1 1/2 cups sugar
3 tablespoons plus 1 teaspoon cornstarch
1/2 teaspoon salt
3 cups milk
6 egg yolks
2 tablespoons unsalted butter
1 tablespoon dark rum
1/2 cup whipping cream
1 banana, sliced
1/2 cup chopped macadamia nuts
1 banana, sliced
1/2 cup whipping cream
1 teaspoon confectioners' sugar
1 teaspoon dark rum

For the crust, preheat the oven to 475 degrees. Combine the macadamia nuts, coconut and brown sugar in a bowl and mix well. Beat the egg white in a mixing bowl until stiff peaks form. Fold into the coconut mixture. Spoon into the pie shell. Cover the pastry edge with strips of foil. Bake for 6 to 7 minutes; remove the foil. Bake for 1 to 3 minutes longer or until golden brown. Let stand until cool.

For the filling, combine the sugar, cornstarch and salt in a saucepan and mix well. Whisk the milk and egg yolks in a bowl just until blended. Add to the sugar mixture and mix well. Cook over medium heat until thickened, stirring constantly. Remove from heat. Stir in the butter and 1 tablespoon rum. Chill, covered, for 2 to 4 hours.

Beat 1/2 cup whipping cream in a mixing bowl until stiff peaks form. Fold into the custard mixture. Arrange 1 sliced banana over the bottom of the prepared pie plate. Spoon the custard over the banana. Sprinkle with the macadamia nuts. Chill, covered, in the refrigerator.

Arrange 1 sliced banana over the top of the pie. Beat 1/2 cup whipping cream in a mixing bowl until soft peaks form. Add the confectioners' sugar and 1 teaspoon rum and mix well. Spread over the top, sealing to the edge. Chill until serving time.

Note: May prepare 12 to 24 hours in advance of serving.

aspberry Ice Cream and
Grapefruit Granita—
Frozen paradise

Blueberry Tart

SERVES 8 TO 10

Processor Crust
2 cups flour
4 teaspoons sugar
1/8 teaspoon salt
1 cup (2 sticks) butter
2 tablespoons white vinegar
Blueberry Filling
1 cup sugar
1/4 cup flour
1/8 teaspoon cinnamon
4 cups fresh blueberries

For the crust, combine the flour, sugar and salt in a food processor fitted with a steel blade. Process until mixed. Add the butter. Process until crumbly. Add the vinegar. Process until blended. Pat into a 12-inch tart pan.

For the filling, preheat the oven to 350 degrees. Combine the sugar, flour and cinnamon in a bowl and mix well. Add 2 cups of the blueberries and toss gently to coat. Spoon into the prepared tart pan. Bake for 1 hour. Sprinkle the remaining 2 cups blueberries over the top of the warm tart and press gently. Let stand until cool. Garnish with confectioners' sugar.

Note: Arrange red raspberries around the outer edge of the tart pan for a colorful presentation at the next Fourth of July celebration. May prepare up to 1 day in advance.

Catawba Peach Tart

SERVES 8 OR 9

Sour Cream Crust
1 1/4 cups flour
2 tablespoons sour cream
1/4 teaspoon salt
1/2 cup (1 stick) butter
Peach Filling
1 quart thinly sliced fresh peaches
1 cup sugar
3 egg yolks
1/3 cup sour cream
1 teaspoon vanilla extract
1/2 teaspoon almond extract
1/4 teaspoon salt

For the crust, preheat the oven to 375 degrees. Combine the flour, sour cream and salt in a bowl and mix well. Cut in the butter until crumbly. Spread the crumb mixture in an 8×8-inch or 9×9-inch baking pan sprayed with nonstick cooking spray. Bake for 20 minutes. Maintain the oven temperature.

For the filling, arrange the peaches over the baked layer. Combine the sugar, egg yolks, sour cream, flavorings and salt in a mixing bowl. Beat at low speed until blended. Spoon over the peaches. Bake for 45 minutes. Let stand until cool.

Apple Orchard Dessert

SERVES 8

Walnut Crust
1 cup flour
1 cup packed brown sugar
1/2 cup (1 stick) butter
1/2 cup chopped walnuts
Apple Filling
2 large apples, sliced
1/4 cup flour
1/4 cup sugar
1/2 teaspoon baking soda
1/2 teaspoon cinnamon
1 cup sour cream
1/4 cup orange marmalade
2 tablespoons lemon juice
1 tablespoon butter, softened
1 egg, lightly beaten

For the crust, preheat the oven to 350 degrees. Combine the flour and brown sugar in a bowl and mix well. Cut in the butter until crumbly. Stir in the walnuts. Pat the crumb mixture over the bottom of a 10-inch springform pan. Bake for 8 minutes or until light brown. Maintain the oven temperature.

For the filling, arrange the apples in an overlapping pattern over the baked layer. Combine the flour, sugar, baking soda and cinnamon in a mixing bowl and mix well. Add the sour cream, marmalade, lemon juice, butter and egg and beat until blended. Spoon over the apples. Bake for 40 minutes. Let stand until cool. Garnish with confectioners' sugar.

Note: May prepare up to 1 day in advance of serving.

Faux Strudel

SERVES 4 TO 6

2 1/4 cups flour, sifted
1 tablespoon sugar
3/4 teaspoon salt
1 cup sour cream
1 cup (2 sticks) butter, melted
8 to 9 ounces orange marmalade
8 to 9 ounces apricot preserves
1 cup finely chopped walnuts
3/4 cup golden raisins
1/2 cup packed brown sugar
2 tablespoons cinnamon

Combine the flour, sugar and salt in a bowl and mix well. Add the sour cream and butter, stirring until the mixture forms a ball. Chill, wrapped in waxed paper, for 2 to 10 hours. Divide the dough into 4 equal portions. Roll each portion into a rectangle on floured waxed paper.

Preheat the oven to 325 degrees. Combine the marmalade and preserves in a bowl and mix well. Spread equal amounts on the 4 rectangles. Combine the walnuts, raisins, brown sugar and cinnamon in a bowl and toss to mix. Sprinkle equal amounts of the walnut mixture over the 4 rectangles. Roll each rectangle as for a jelly roll to enclose filling.

Arrange the rolls on a greased and floured baking sheet. Bake for 1 hour. Remove to a wire rack to cool. Cut each roll into 9 slices. Garnish with confectioners' sugar just before serving. Arrange the slices on a serving platter.

Flourless Chocolate Cake

SERVES 8

Cake
4 ounces semisweet chocolate
$1/2$ cup (1 stick) unsalted butter
$2/3$ cup sugar
Grated zest of 1 orange
1 tablespoon Grand Marnier
3 eggs
2 cups ground walnuts
Chocolate Glaze
6 ounces semisweet chocolate
6 tablespoons unsalted butter
1 tablespoon light corn syrup

For the cake, preheat the oven to 375 degrees. Coat the side and bottom of a 9-inch cake pan with butter and dust lightly with flour. Line the bottom with waxed paper.

Combine the chocolate and $1/2$ cup butter in a double boiler over simmering water. Cook until blended, stirring frequently. Add the sugar and orange zest and mix well.

Cook until the sugar dissolves, stirring constantly. Remove from heat.

Let stand for 5 minutes. Stir in the Grand Marnier. Add the eggs 1 at a time, mixing well after each addition. Stir in the walnuts. Spoon the batter into the prepared pan. Bake for 25 to 30 minutes or until the cake tests done; do not overbake. Remove to a wire rack to cool.

For the glaze, combine the chocolate and butter in a saucepan. Cook over low heat until blended, stirring constantly. Stir in the corn syrup. Cook until of a glaze consistency, stirring constantly. Drizzle over the cake. Garnish with walnut halves.

Note: May prepare up to 1 day in advance of serving.

Glacé Emeraude

SERVES 6

3 cups water
$1 2/3$ cups sugar
$1/2$ cup fresh lemon juice
$1/4$ cup crème de menthe
Green food coloring

Combine the water and sugar in a saucepan and mix well. Bring to a boil. Boil for 10 minutes, stirring occasionally. Let stand until cool. Stir in the lemon juice, crème de menthe and several drops of green food coloring. Pour into a glass container. Freeze, covered, in the freezer, until firm, stirring twice. Spoon into dessert goblets.

Grapefruit Granita

SERVES 8

4 cups fresh grapefruit juice, at room temperature
1 cup superfine sugar

Combine the grapefruit juice and sugar in a bowl and stir until the sugar dissolves. Pour into a shallow dish. Freeze for 5 hours or until the mixture is entirely crystallized, stirring every hour to scrape the crystals from the edges of the dish. Mash the frozen mixture with a potato masher or process in a food processor until the ice has a slightly granular texture 30 minutes before serving. Spoon into dessert goblets. Garnish with edible flowers or sprigs of fresh mint.

Note: May prepare up to 2 days in advance of serving.

Frozen Grand Marnier Soufflé

SERVES 8

Soufflé
1 quart vanilla ice cream, softened
4 macaroons, crushed
1/2 cup Grand Marnier
1 cup whipping cream, stiffly beaten
1/4 cup chopped almonds
Sugar to taste
Strawberry Sauce
1/4 cup confectioners' sugar
1 quart fresh strawberries, or 20 ounces frozen strawberries
1/2 cup Grand Marnier

For the soufflé, combine the ice cream, macaroons and Grand Marnier in a bowl and mix well. Fold in the whipped cream. Spoon the ice cream mixture into a 6-cup mold. Sprinkle with the almonds and sugar. Freeze, covered, for 8 to 10 hours.

For the sauce, combine the confectioners' sugar and strawberries in a saucepan. Bring to a boil over medium heat, stirring frequently; reduce heat. Cook until the strawberries are tender but not mushy, stirring frequently. Remove from heat. Stir in the Grand Marnier. Cover to keep warm.

To serve, wrap the mold in a hot towel for 4 to 5 seconds. Loosen the edge and invert the mold onto a chilled serving platter. Serve with the warm sauce.

Danish Almond Pudding

SERVES 8

Pudding
2 envelopes unflavored gelatin
1/4 cup cold water
2 cups light cream
2 cups milk
7 egg yolks
1/4 cup sugar
1 cup chopped almonds, lightly toasted
2 tablespoons almond extract
Raspberry Sauce
1 jar raspberry jelly
1/4 cup hot water
1 tablespoon butter
1 tablespoon flour

For the pudding, soften the gelatin in the cold water in a saucepan. Cook over low heat until dissolved, stirring frequently. Stir in the light cream and milk. Bring to a boil, stirring constantly. Beat the egg yolks and sugar in a mixing bowl until thickened. Add to the cream mixture and mix well. Cook until thickened, stirring constantly; do not boil. Let stand until cool. Stir in the almonds and flavoring. Spoon into 8 pot de crème cups. Chill until serving time.

For the sauce, heat the jelly in a saucepan until melted. Stir in the hot water, butter and flour. Cook until of the desired consistency, stirring constantly. Chill, covered, in the refrigerator. Serve with the pudding.

Lemon Bread Pudding

SERVES 6

1/4 cup (1/2 stick) butter
3 tablespoons lemon juice
Grated zest of 1 lemon
1 cup sugar
3 eggs, lightly beaten
8 slices bread, crusts trimmed
1 cup milk
3 tablespoons sugar
2 eggs, lightly beaten
Grated zest of 1 lemon
1/8 teaspoon salt

Combine the butter, lemon juice and zest of 1 lemon in a saucepan. Cook for 2 minutes, stirring frequently. Stir in 1 cup sugar and 3 eggs. Cook over low heat until thickened, stirring constantly. Let stand until cool.

Spread the bread slices with the lemon mixture. Arrange in a buttered 8×8-inch baking dish. Whisk the milk, 3 tablespoons sugar, 2 eggs, zest of 1 lemon and salt in a bowl. Pour over the prepared layers.

Let stand at room temperature for 15 minutes or in the refrigerator for a longer amount of time. Bake at 350 degrees for 1 hour.

Summer Pudding

SERVES 8

1 pint strawberries
1 pint raspberries
1 pint blueberries
1 pint red or black currants
1/2 cup sugar
1 (1-pound) brioche, crusts trimmed
1/3 cup framboise or any fruit-flavored wine
1 1/2 cups whipping cream
1 teaspoon grated orange zest

Mash the strawberries, raspberries, blueberries and currants lightly in a bowl and sprinkle with the sugar. Let stand for 1 hour or until the berries have produced 3/4 cup juice. Drain, reserving the juice.

Cut the brioche into 1/2-inch slices. Line the side and bottom of a 2-quart soufflé dish with some of the slices. Combine the reserved berry juice and framboise in a bowl and mix well. Brush the bread with the berry juice mixture just until moistened.

Beat the whipping cream in a mixing bowl until soft peaks form. Fold into the berry mixture. Stir in the orange zest. Spoon the fruit mixture into the prepared soufflé dish. Cut the remaining bread into squares and arrange over the top of the fruit mixture. Cover with plastic wrap. Place a plate over the top to weigh down the pudding. Chill for 24 hours. Invert onto a serving platter. Garnish with edible flowers.

Note: May also use blackberries and gooseberries in this pudding.

Mother's Gingerbread

SERVES 10 TO 12

Gingerbread

2¹/2 cups flour
2 teaspoons cinnamon
1¹/2 teaspoons baking soda
1 teaspoon ground cloves
1 teaspoon ground ginger
1 cup (2 sticks) butter, softened
1 cup sugar
3 egg yolks
1 cup molasses
1 cup water
3 egg whites

Orange Whipped Cream

2 cups whipping cream
Confectioners' sugar to taste
Orange liqueur to taste
Grated orange zest to taste

For the gingerbread, preheat the oven to 350 degrees. Sift the flour, cinnamon, baking soda, cloves and ginger together. Beat the butter and sugar in a mixing bowl until creamy, scraping the bowl occasionally. Add the egg yolks 1 at a time, mixing well after each addition. Add the molasses and water and mix well. Stir in the flour mixture.

Beat the egg whites in a mixing bowl until stiff peaks form. Fold into the batter. Spoon the batter into 24 muffin cups or a 2-quart mold. Bake the muffins for 20 minutes or until a wooden pick inserted in the centers comes out clean or for 35 to 40 minutes for the mold.

For the cream, beat the whipping cream in a mixing bowl until soft peaks form. Add the desired amount of confectioners' sugar, orange liqueur and orange zest and mix well. Serve with the gingerbread.

Note: May store the batter, covered, in the refrigerator for up to 1 week.

This work of studio glass rewards the viewer with delicious details. A conspicuously dropped napkin suggests the hurried departure of a customer following a meal of meat loaf, mashed potatoes, and homemade pie.

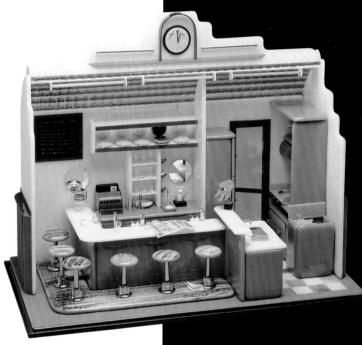

Emily Brock
American, born 1945

THE COUNTERMAN-DINER
Glass, 1991–1992

Purchased with funds given in memory of Judie Chatreau by friends and co-workers at Society Bank & Trust, and with funds from the Libbey Endowment, Gift of Edward Drummond Libbey

Melon Ball Cocktail

SERVES 6

1 cup dry white wine
1/4 cup honey
4 cups fresh (3/4-inch) melon balls
24 red raspberries
1 bottle Champagne

Pour a mixture of the white wine and honey over the melon balls in a bowl and toss gently to coat. Marinate, covered with plastic wrap, in the refrigerator for 2 hours or longer; drain.

Divide the melon balls equally among 6 chilled 8-ounce goblets. Top each serving with 4 raspberries. Fill the goblets with Champagne. Garnish with fresh mint leaves.

Note: The melon balls can either be one variety of melon or an assortment, depending on taste and availability of varieties of melons.

Frozen Mocha Mousse

SERVES 16 TO 20

3 tablespoons instant coffee granules
1/2 cup boiling water
1 pound semisweet chocolate
6 egg yolks
1/2 cup sugar
1 teaspoon vanilla extract
6 egg whites
1 1/2 cups whipping
1/2 cup whipping cr

USES ~~EGGS~~

Dissolve the coffee gran... boiling water. Cool slightly. Heat the chocolate in a double boiler over hot water until melted, stirring occasionally.

Beat the egg yolks in a mixing bowl at high speed until foamy. Add the sugar gradually, beating constantly until thick and pale yellow. Add the coffee, chocolate and vanilla. Beat at medium speed until blended.

Beat the egg whites in a mixing bowl until stiff peaks form. Stir 1 cup of the beaten egg whites into the chocolate mixture. Stir the chocolate mixture into the egg whites. Fold in 1 1/2 cups whipped cream. Spoon into an 8-inch springform pan. Freeze, covered, until firm, or for up to 1 month.

To serve, remove the mousse from the freezer 20 to 25 minutes before serving. Remove the side of the pan and place on a serving platter. Mound 1/2 cup whipped cream over the top of the mousse. Garnish with chocolate curls.

Boca Negra

SERVES 8 TO 10

White Chocolate Cream

12 ounces white chocolate, finely chopped
1 cup heavy cream
1/4 cup Chambord (Black Raspberry Liqueur)

Cake

12 ounces European bittersweet chocolate, coarsely chopped
1 cup sugar
1/2 cup Chambord
1 cup (2 sticks) unsalted butter, cut into 10 pieces, softened
5 large eggs, at room temperature
1/3 cup sugar
1 1/2 tablespoons flour

For the cream, place the white chocolate in the work bowl of a food processor fitted with a steel blade. Heat the heavy cream in a saucepan until small bubbles form around the edge of the pan. Pour the hot whipping cream over the chocolate. Process until smooth. Add the liqueur. Process until blended. Taste and add up to 1 tablespoon additional liqueur if desired. Chill, covered, for 8 to 10 hours.

For the cake, preheat the oven to 350 degrees. Position a rack in the center of the oven. Coat a 9-inch cake pan lightly with butter. Line the bottom with parchment paper. Place the pan in a shallow roasting pan.

Place the chocolate in a bowl. Combine 1 cup sugar and the liqueur in a saucepan. Cook over medium heat until the sugar dissolves and the mixture comes to a boil, stirring occasionally. Pour over the chocolate and stir with a spatula until the mixture is smooth. Add the butter 1 piece at a time, mixing until blended after each addition.

Whisk the eggs and 1/3 cup sugar in a bowl until slightly thickened. Whisk into the chocolate mixture until blended. Whisk in the flour gently. Spoon the batter into the prepared pan. Add just enough hot water to the roasting pan to reach 1 inch up the side of the cake pan. Bake for exactly 30 minutes; the top will have a dry thin crust. Remove the cake from the water bath and wipe the pan dry. Cover the top of the cake with plastic wrap. Invert onto a plate and discard the parchment paper. Invert onto a serving platter and remove the plastic wrap. Serve warm or at room temperature with the chilled white chocolate cream.

Note: May store, covered with plastic wrap, at room temperature for up to 1 day or in the refrigerator for up to 3 days. May be stored, wrapped in foil, in the freezer for up to 1 month. Thaw in the refrigerator. Serve at room temperature or reheat just until warm.

Chocolate Pears

SERVES 6

Pears

$1/4$ to $1/2$ cup sugar, or to taste

5 cups water

Juice of 1 lemon

2 cinnamon sticks

4 whole cloves

6 firm Bosc pears with stems

4 ounces unsweetened chocolate

2 ounces semisweet chocolate

$1/4$ cup ($1/2$ stick) butter, softened

Crème Anglaise

2 cups heavy cream

$1/4$ cup sugar

1 teaspoon vanilla extract

6 egg yolks, beaten

For the pears, dissolve the sugar in the water in a large saucepan. Stir in the lemon juice, cinnamon sticks and cloves. Simmer, covered, for 15 minutes or until of a syrupy consistency, stirring occasionally. Place the pears in an upright position in the syrup. Poach for 30 to 40 minutes or until the pears are tender but firm. Let stand until cool. Chill, covered, in the syrup for 8 to 10 hours; drain.

Combine the unsweetened chocolate, semisweet chocolate and butter in a double boiler over hot water. Cook until blended, stirring frequently. Pat the pears dry. Dip the pears by the stems into the chocolate, turning to coat. Arrange stem side up on a platter. Chill until set or for up to 24 hours.

For the sauce, combine the heavy cream, sugar and vanilla in a saucepan and mix well. Bring to a boil, stirring frequently. Stir half the hot mixture into the egg yolks. Stir the egg yolks into the hot mixture. Cook for 5 minutes or until thickened, stirring constantly. Chill, covered, in the refrigerator.

To serve, puddle the Crème Anglaise on each of 6 dessert plates. Place the pears in the center of the sauce.

Raspberry Walnut Torte

SERVES 8 TO 10

1 (12-ounce) package frozen raspberries, thawed

1 cup flour

$1/3$ cup confectioners' sugar

$1/3$ cup butter, softened

$3/4$ cup chopped walnuts

1 cup sugar

$1/4$ cup flour

2 eggs

1 teaspoon vanilla extract

$1/2$ teaspoon salt

$1/2$ teaspoon baking powder

$1/2$ cup sugar

$1/2$ cup water

2 tablespoons cornstarch

Preheat the oven to 350 degrees. Drain the raspberries, reserving the juice. Combine 1 cup flour and confectioners' sugar in a bowl and mix well. Cut in the butter until crumbly. Press into an ungreased 9-inch springform pan. Bake for 15 minutes. Let stand until cool. Sprinkle the raspberries and walnuts over the baked layer.

Beat the sugar, $1/4$ cup flour, eggs, vanilla, salt and baking powder in a mixing bowl at low speed until blended. Spoon into the prepared pan. Bake for 35 to 40 minutes or until golden brown. Let stand until cool.

Combine the reserved raspberry juice, sugar, water and cornstarch in a saucepan. Cook until thick and clear, stirring constantly. Let stand until cool.

To serve, remove the side of the pan. Drizzle the sauce over the top of the torte. Cut into wedges. Garnish each serving with whipped cream, additional raspberries and mint leaves.

Plum Torte

SERVES 8 TO 12

³/4 cup sugar
¹/2 cup (1 stick)
1 cup unbleache
1 teaspoon baki
¹/8 teaspoon sa
2 eggs
12 purple plun
2 tablespoons suga
1 tablespoon lemon juice
¹/2 teaspoon cinnamon, or to taste

looks good

Preheat the oven to 350 degrees. Beat ³/4 cup sugar and butter in a mixing bowl until creamy, scraping the bowl occasionally. Add the flour, baking powder, salt and eggs. Beat until blended. Spoon the batter into an 8-, 9- or 10-inch springform pan. Arrange the plum halves skin side up over the top. Sprinkle with 2 tablespoons sugar and drizzle with the lemon juice. Sprinkle with the cinnamon. Bake for 1 hour. Cool in pan on a wire rack. Serve plain or with whipped cream.

Raspberry Ice Cream

SERVES 4

2 pints fresh raspberries
1 cup sugar, or to taste
1 cup whipping cream
2 tablespoons Cointreau or any liqueur

Process the raspberries in a blender until puréed. Strain into a bowl, discarding the seeds.

Combine the raspberry purée, sugar, whipping cream and liqueur in a bowl and mix well. Pour into an ice cream freezer container. Freeze using the manufacturer's directions.

Café Finale

SERVES 6

1 cup Cognac
1 cup brandy
1 cup coffee liqueur
1 cup extra-strong coffee
1 lemon, cut into halves
¹/4 cup superfine sugar
1 cup whipping cream, whipped
¹/8 teaspoon cinnamon
1 tablespoon grated dark chocolate

Combine the Cognac, brandy, coffee liqueur and coffee in a pitcher and stir gently. Let stand at room temperature for 8 hours or longer. Rub the rims of 6 microwave-safe burgundy wine goblets with the lemon. Dip the moist rims into the sugar and gently shake out any excess sugar that has fallen into the goblets.

Stir the Cognac mixture gently and pour into the goblets. Microwave on High just until the coffee begins to boil. Top each with whipped cream. Sprinkle with the cinnamon and chocolate. Serve immediately.

COMMITTEES

Chairman:
Marilyn Arbaugh

Steering Committee:
Skipper Christen
Barbara Cummins
Phyllis Ide

Business Chairman:
Ursula Barrett

Committee:
Anita Daverio
Linda Pawlecki
June Roshe
Barbara Thierwechter
Karen Uebelhart

Computer Chairman:
Leslie McCaffery

Committee:
Janell Falter
Carol Kistler
Andrea Monoky

Editorial Cochairmen:
Ellie Brunner
Lois Burke

Committee:
Nancy Beren
Susie Cohn
Tibble Foster
Phyllis Ide
Sandra Knudsen (Museum Staff)
Lynne Lippman
Jean McMillan
Sharmon Minns
Carol Orser
Susan Palmer (Museum Staff)
Nan Plummer (Museum Staff)

Art and Design Chairman:
Stacey Kripke

Committee:
Susan Carr
Patti Coffin
Barbara Coon
Dora Crowther
Sally Giauque
Elaine Green
Nita Harrington
Ann Jane Hileman
Barbara McKelvy
Carol Pletz
Nancy Quandt
Susan Reams
Suzanne Rorick
Dee Wainstein

Marketing & Sales Cochairmen:
Diane Churdar
Diane Miller

Committee:
Kay Ball
Cecile Bennett
Anita Daverio
Maureen Donovan
Carol Fox
Carol Geracioti
Ruth Hanson
Jane Keller
Martha Kudner
Peggy Lewis
Doris McEwen
Diane Phillips
Marilyn Rinehart
Nathalie Ryan
Ruth Ann Sailstad
Katie Schueler
Jeanie Silletti
Vickie Souder
Lillian Spaulding
Wanda Tyo
Jo Ann Winzeler

Funding and Underwriting Chairman:
Diane Phillips

Committee:

Nancy Ankney
Carol Bardi
Nancy Beren
Jeanette Bradley
Ellie Brunner
Susan Carr
Deborah Chapman
Patti Coffin
Barbara Cummins
Maureen Donovan
Nancy Fairhurst
Faye Fenwick
Barbara Goldberg
Tracy Jamieson
Stacey Kripke
Judy Lonergan
Judy Mainwold
Diane Miller
Leslie McCaffery

Carol Orser
LaNelle Rhodes
Sandra Sloan
Peg Smith
Ica Sutter
Eddy Cobau Taylor
Margy Trumbull
Ina Tuschman
Joan Vicinus
Sue White
Val Wiley
Karen Uebelhart

Food Committee Chairman:
Pamela Straub

Committee:

Nancy Ankney
Kay Ball
Carol Bardi
Cecile Bennett
Deborah Chapman
Diane Churdar
Judy Cohen
Suzanne Cook
Anita Daverio
Carol Fox
Carol Geracioti
Ruth Hanson
Chris Hartman
Nancy Kabat
Titi Kakissis
Irene Kaufman
Shari Kellermeyer
Doris McEwen
Diane Miller
Marian Moore
Lindy Munn
Donna Niehous
Linda Pawlecki
Suzanne Petti
LaNelle Rhodes
Diane Snyder
Sue Speck
Joelyn Stone

SPONSORS

Dick and Fran Anderson
Appliance Center of Toledo, Inc.
Calphalon Corporation
Libbey Inc.

Arlington Rack & Packaging
Roger M. and Rhoda L. Berkowitz
Ellie and Jim Brunner
Mr. and Mrs. Fred Christen
Dana Corporation
Tony and Mary Lou Falzone, SPL, Inc.
Phyllis G. Ide
Stacey and Harley Kripke
Mancy's Steaks/Mancy's Italian
Leslie and Joseph McCaffery
Owens-Illinois, Inc.

Marilyn and Jim Arbaugh
Carol and Edward Bardi
Beirut and Byblos Restaurants
Lois and Michael Burke
Diane and Paul Churdar
Suzanne T. Cohn
Cousino's Navy Bistro
Mr. and Mrs. Paul V. Daverio
Eastman & Smith Ltd.
Greg and Helen Emmert
Tibble Foster
Mr. and Mrs. Robert M. Fox, Jr.
John and Barbara Hammill
Harold Jaffe Jewelers, Inc.
Nancy Kabat, Welles Bowen Realtors
Mr. and Mrs. Dean P. Kasperzak
Diane and Bill Miller
The Moses-Schlachter Group, Inc.
Ohio Belting and Transmission
Diane and Jerome Phillips
Premier Steel Inc.
Romanoff Electric Corporation
Robert E. and Anne C. Schwertfeger
Mr. and Mrs. Philip G. Simonds
Mr. and Mrs. John L. Straub
Thackeray's Books
Mrs. Erma K. Zerner
Nancy Zerner

Atlas World Travel
Cecile Renuart Bennett
Thomas N. and Gill W. Bentley
Carol Bintz
Emma Leah Bippus
Dee and Jim Blumer
Coldwell Banker Premier Realty
Deborah Chapman
Judy Cohen
Mrs. Suzanne C. Cook
Courts of Sylvania/Westowne
    Tennis Clubs
Barbara and Jim Cummins
Jeff and Sally DePerro
Tom and Nancy Fairhurst
Fifi's Restaurant
Sanda and Jim Findley
Georgio's Café International
Dr. and Mrs. Thomas Geracioti
Mr. and Mrs. John N. Graham
Edna and George Hammond
Don and Darla Harbaugh
Mr. and Mrs. Paul F. Heymann
Anne D. Hirsch
Mr. and Mrs. Richard C. Howe
Tracy A. Jamieson
Mr. and Mrs. Newell Kaufman
Shari Kellermeyer
Kitchen Design Plus
Lathrop Company
Mr. and Mrs. Walter W. Lathrop
The Legacy Restaurant
Robert and Judy Lonergan
Jean and Jim MacMillan
Meyer Hill Lynch Corporation
Judith Milano
Sue Mueller
Mr. and Mrs. William O.
    Murtagh

Noral Realtors
O'Briens Refrigeration & Air
    Conditioning Service
Sam Okun Produce Company
Mrs. Peter Orser
Owens Corning
Mr. and Mrs. Dennis Pawlecki
Susan Pennell
Tom and Carol Pletz
Pugh Heating & Air
    Conditioning Company
Suzanne and J. B. Rorick
Betty Rumpf Interiors, Inc.
Nathalie M. Ryan
Phil, Darryl, and Gary Sahadi
    Family
Ellie and George Seifried
Gayle Sparagowski
Lillian Spaulding
Millard and Joelyn Stone
Spencer and Prudy Stone
Styl-Rite Lampshades
Ica and Jerry Sutter
Eddy and Doug Taylor
Barbara Thierwechter
Margy and Scott Trumbull
Mr. and Mrs. Lance Tyo
USA Baby of Toledo
Jean and Frank Voss
Deanna and Mayer Wainstein
J. D. Wesley's Bistro
Westgate Bassetts Health Foods
John C. Westoven,
    Cavalear Insurance
Jo Ann Winzeler
Sandra Wiseley
Ann C. Witte
Roger E. Wyman

Acme Detroit Saw
Mr. and Mrs. Richard W. and
    Loviah E. Aldinger
Cynthia and Jim Apostolakis
Kay Ball
Jim and Ursula Barrett
The Berman Building Company
Mr. and Mrs. C. James Carr
Central Travel
Closettec
Barbara and Robert Coon
Mrs. Malcolm Crowther
Croy's Supper Club, Inc.
Maureen Donovan
First Class Reunions &
    Events, Inc.
J. Foster Jewelers
Mrs. O. L. Giauque
Elaine and Don Green
Fred and Nita Harrington
Gary and Chris Hartman
Mr. and Mrs. Edward Hiett
Marjorie S. Hunter
Mr. and Mrs. Ross Keller
Tom Keller, One Day Sign
Ken's Flower Shops
Martha and Dick Kudner
Jim Loss, Loss Realty Group
Mainline Kitchen and Bath
    Design Center
Mr. and Mrs. James G. Marriott
Matthew's Creative Cuisine
Doris and Jim McEwen
Patricia McNerney
Sharmon M. Minns
Mrs. Hollis A. Moore
Mr. and Mrs. Patrick Moore

Bill and Lindy Munn
Donna and Bill Niehous
Parker Steel Company
Jill Peterson
Nancy Quandt
Real Property Analysts
Dr. and Mrs. Donald Rinehart
Mrs. Richard T. Rudduck
Nancy and Alan Rudolph
Sautter's Food Center
Dr. and Mrs. Charles K. Sawyer
Jeanie Silletti
Sandra Phillips Sloan
Mike and Peg Smith
Jeanean Snow, ReMax Masters
Vickie Souder
Swang's Carpet Cleaning
Today's Lighting by Phyllis &
    Company
Toledo Furs, Inc.
Chris Trellis Builders
Mr. and Mrs. James Tuschman
Karen Uebelhart
Walker Funeral Home
Jane Wurth, Welles Bowen
    Realtors

CONTRIBUTORS

Nancy Ankney
Marilyn Arbaugh
Joan Arnos
Kay Ball
Carol Bardi
Marj Baril
John A. Barrett, Jr.
Ursula Barrett
Cecile Bennett
Gill Bentley
Nancy Beren
Rhoda Berkowitz
Carol Bintz
Dee Blumer
Molly Boeschenstein
Mary Boyd
Jeanette Bradley
Margot Brauer
Paula Brown
Sandra Brown
Lois Burke
Susan Carr
Deborah Chapman
Skipper Christen
Diane Churdar
Patti Coffin
Judy Cohen
Clair Cole
Suzanne Cook
Barbara Coon
Dora Crowther
Barbara Cummins
Anita Daverio
Judy Dye
Molly Ehni
Helen Emmert

Nancy Fairhurst
Janell Falter
Tibble Foster
Wanda Foster
Carol Fox
Patricia Frechette
Carol Geracioti
Sally Giauque
Barbara Goldberg
Elaine Green
Ruth Hanson
Mary Jo Hardy
Nita Harrington
Chris Hartman
Nancy Heymann
Margie Hiett
Ann Jane Hileman
Barbara Hoversten
Posy Huebner
Marge Hunter
Phyllis Ide
Tracy Jamieson
Nancy Kabat
Titi Kakissis
Irene Kaufman
Jane Keller
Shari Kellermeyer
Carol Kistler
J.J. Kosmider
Stacey Kripke
Martha Kudner
Anne Lathrop
Peggy Lewis
Judy Lonergan
Suzanne Loos
Gretchen Lyon

Jean MacMillan
Judy Mainwold
Jean Marriott
Leslie McCaffery
Jeanne McElheney
Doris McEwen
Barbara McKelvy
Kathy McKimmy
Mary Alice McKone
Pat McNerney
Diane Miller
Sharmon Minns
Andrea Monoky
Kitty Moore
Marian Moore
Sue Mueller
Lindy Munn
Carol Nichols
Donna Niehous
Ann O'Leary
Carol Orser
Susan Palmer
Linda Pawlecki
Sue Pennell
Suzanne Petti
Diane Phillips
Carol Pletz
Nancy Quandt
Janet Raddatz
Katie Raddatz
Susan Reams
LaNelle Rhodes
Marilyn Rinehart
Suzanne Rorick
June Roshe
Nancy Rudolph

Nathalie Ryan
Ruth Ann Sailstad
Ann Sawyer
Katie Schueler
Brooke Simonds
Sandra Sloan
Lois Slotterbeck
Melissa Smith
Diane Snyder
Vickie Souder
Lillian Spaulding
Sue Speck
Penny Staelin
Kathy Steadman
Karen Stevens
Joelyn Stone
Pamela Straub
Ica Sutter
Christine Swenson
Eddy Cobau Taylor
Barbara Thierwechter
Margy Trumbull
Ina Tuschman
Wanda Tyo
Karen Uebelhart
Jean Voss
Dee Wainstein
Lucy Jane Webster
Patty Westmeyer
Sue White
Jo Ann Winzeler
Sandy Wiseley
Ann Witte
Jacquey Yocum
Nancy Zerner
Mary Zraik

INDEX

L. David Pietro Paulo Rubens H. Matisse
Winslow Homer Bierstadt mary
modigliani J. Jor-f W: van de velde
Picasso Th. Gainsborough Benton Eug Delacro
Frederic Remington
Miró Rembrandt Claude M
Le Brun Joshua Reynolds Piet Mondri
Vincent van Marguer
Yves Tanguy f Boucher Jackson Pollock
Cole P. Cezanne A. VAN DYCK G. Cour
A. Wyeth J. F. Cropsey H. Matis
Homer Benton Pietro Paulo Rubens mary
Th. Gainsborough J. Jor-f Bierstadt
Frederic Remington L. David W: van de velde
Piet Mondriaan Joshua Reynolds Claude Mo
G. Courbet Yves Tanguy
Th. Gainsborough van Marguer